Julia

MY NAME IS BELOVED

May you come to know
Just how loved you are
by Jesus

Mary
x

First published in 2021 by
New Life Publishing, Luton,
Bedfordshire LU3 4DQ

© Mary Hardiman

British Library Cataloguing in Publication Data
A catalogue record for this book is available
from the British Library.

ISBN 978 1 912237 35 7

Typesetting by New Life Publishing,
Luton, UK www.goodnewsbooks.co.uk
Printed and bound in Great Britain

MY NAME IS BELOVED

BELOVED

Bringing the scriptures alive

MARY HARDIMAN

For my Jesus friend,
Ann-Marie Reid.
"Hold up a light."

CONTENTS

RECOMMENDATIONS

Like many people, I am always looking for new authors to inspire and encourage me. Mary Hardiman is just such a one. Her first book 'My Name is Beloved' is a wonderful collection of biblical reflections, full of life, colour, vibrancy and energy. Characters from ancient stories come to life and somehow get into your very soul as their stories are told in a fresh way, with new insight. I felt at times as though they were telling my story as I wrestled with feelings and emotions that emerged within me as I read.

Mary's points for reflection are well thought out and are both encouraging and challenging. They made me stop and think and pray. This is a wonderful book, which I would recommend to anyone and I hope it is the first of many.

Father Chris Thomas

This is Mary Hardiman's first book, so when I received it I was not sure what to expect. To my great delight, I loved her style and way of writing, and when I started reading it I did not want to put it down.

Her choice of Scripture passages is excellent, a new one for every chapter, with a very realistic analysis of the main messages contained in each. Her reflections are helpful, easy to follow, and she makes challenging choices of the areas of focus for the subsequent questions and prayer. This book will help anyone wanting to understand more of the New Testament.

The questions Mary raises throughout the book always demand serious responses from the reader, for example: 'With every gospel passage there are always two questions to ask ourselves. What is this telling us about God? What is this telling us about discipleship?' Then further on she reminds and challenges us: 'We forget that we are all made by God and that there is nothing he cannot put right. Not one thing. Do we believe this? Can we approach that throne of sublime grace willingly and with confidence?' Questions like these are hard to set aside!

This book in its elegant and easy to read format will help every reader to become more familiar with some key Scriptures, and to grow spiritually by applying them to his or her life through the guided reflections and challenging questions.

Charles Whitehead, KSG

INTRODUCTION

IN THE SUMMER OF 2016 I ATTENDED A WEEK OF GUIDED PRAYER at my home parish of St Peter's in Hazel Grove, Stockport. Sometime during that week, my prayer guide Celia and I were discussing names and their meaning. We spoke about my name, her name and what I would have called a daughter, had I had one. Then, out of nowhere Celia asked me a question that changed my life. She asked, 'If you had a God name, what would your God name be?' Before I had given the matter a second's thought, the answer came out of my mouth: 'Beloved, my name is Beloved.'

In Matthew's gospel, (Matthew 3:17) after Jesus is baptised by John in the River Jordan, a voice is heard from heaven, 'This is my son, the beloved, in whom I am well pleased.'

When Jesus is transfigured on the mountain in front of Peter, James and John, the voice of the Father is heard, 'This is my beloved son, listen to him' (Luke 9:35).

We are, all of us, beloved children of God. There have been many times in my life when I have doubted this reality, when I have thought that God could not possibly love me or delight in me. There have also been times when I have heard the voice of God whisper these words, 'You are my beloved' and, somewhere deep within me, I have known this to be true.

Whenever my spiritual life takes a tumble, I remind myself of that conversation with Celia and the words that I said. My name is Beloved.

God's love does not depend on our actions, words or emotions. It does not depend on our successes, our bank balance, our home, our job or our social standing. It doesn't matter where we live, what our skin colour, religion, gender, sexuality, age or marital status is. We can't earn God's love because it's a gift so freely given to all of us, no matter who we are or what we have done. Each of us is his beloved and his favour rests on us.

As you journey through this book with me, my prayer is that you will hear the still, small voice of our mighty God telling you that you are his beloved, that nothing you could ever do or fail to do will change that. I pray that you will be comforted, encouraged, strengthened, held, challenged and, most especially, surprised by this incredible, inclusive and outrageous love, poured out for you. You, too, are God's beloved and his favour rests on you.

PART ONE

GET READY

1. *JESUS TALKS OF BLAZING FIRE*

Jesus said to his disciples: 'I have come to bring fire to the earth, and how I wish it were blazing already! There is a baptism I must still receive, and how great is my distress till it is over!

'Do you suppose that I am here to bring peace on earth? No, I tell you, but rather division. For from now on a household of five will be divided: three against two and two against three, the father divided against the son, son against father, mother against daughter, daughter against mother, mother-in-law against daughter-in-law, daughter-in-law against mother-in-law.'
(Luke 12:49-53)

REFLECTION

When I was growing up we used to have a coal fire in our living room. My job was to roll up the old newspapers to start the fire and my older brothers would bring in the sticks and coal for mum or dad to light it. I used to love watching the fire take hold and to see the flames leap and dance before the coal went on and the fire became somehow calmer and stronger.

What does Jesus mean when he says that he has come to bring fire to the earth and that he wishes it were blazing already? What does he mean when he says that there is a baptism still to be received and how great is his distress until it is over?

I think that Jesus is talking about his death and resurrection, after which the disciples would receive the baptism of the Holy Spirit, a baptism of fire which would transform a disparate, frightened group into powerhouses of God's mercy and grace. I believe that Jesus wanted to see his disciples leap and dance with the joy of God's Holy Spirit, like a blazing fire taking hold.

This baptism of fire would embolden his disciples; it would give them a divine authority to do what Jesus did and more. This baptism would empower his followers to preach with a conviction so audacious that over 2,000 years later, from an ordinary home in Northwest England, some 2,377 miles from Jerusalem, a woman would sit at a desk and write that same message for you to read – the message of God's love. How amazing is that?

No longer would Jesus' disciples need the parables to be explained to them over and over again; no longer would they be arguing about which of them is the greatest and trying to reserve the best seats of glory in heaven. No longer would these men be shooing the children away or failing to comprehend the mission of Christ. I'm not surprised that Jesus couldn't wait for it to be over! Who wouldn't?

Don't forget too that creating Christianity out of Judaism was never going to be an easy ride. There will always be some who resist change. Familial strife was unavoidable. Even today families can be divided as some respond to the call of God whilst others remain hostile and unreceptive.

Where do you sit on this? Is there religious strife in your family? Do you struggle with that? I have heard parents lament the fact that their children no longer go to church or avail themselves of the sacraments. I have heard many people tell me that their family members are 'over religious' and that they often feel suffocated and unable to express or reveal their true selves for fear of judgement and criticism.

And so the overwhelming message of love becomes even more important when we live among those whose views differ from ours. To refrain from judgement and to show love as Jesus did should be our ultimate goal. A tough message for sure!

What does a baptism of fire mean? In this day and age, we use this term to describe a difficult introduction to a new job or activity. We may also refer to this experience as being 'thrown in at the deep end'. When this happens to us, we often feel disorientated, inadequate or even afraid. We can even feel that the task is beyond us.

What we have to remember was that Jesus was fully divine and fully human. It's difficult to see Jesus as 'distressed' when he always seems so sure of himself.

Feelings of fear and inadequacy can distress us and I'm certain that everyone can empathise with these emotions.

No doubt Jesus' ministry must have felt a bit like that at times and so I wonder if he would have longed for his friends to shoulder that burden of ignition with him.

And again, maybe there is a message for us too. Do we need the love and support of others when it comes to faith sharing? Are we able to sustain our family and friends when they struggle with division and separation? Do we listen without judgement? Can we ask for help from our community with humility and modesty? Do we need to pray for the grace to do this?

That's perhaps the more straightforward bit of this gospel text. The second half, however, seems a bit bewildering to me. I don't know about you, but I always thought that Jesus did come to bring unity and peace. Don't we sometimes sing the hymn, 'We are one in the Spirit, we are one in the Lord'? Here, he seems to contradict that. Yet, if we look at the whole of Jesus' ministry and mission, it's not that complicated.

The gospels tell us who Christ is. He is the human face of God the Father; Jesus came to show us the love of our Heavenly Father. And this love is for everyone, even those we find difficult to love. In every encounter, in every parable we see this love reaching out to those in positions of authority and to those on the margins of society. Jesus loves the beggars, the thieves, the prostitutes, the sick, disabled and disfigured. But he also loves the scribes, the Pharisees and the temple guards. He even loved those who put him to death. And he calls us to do the same.

So the division Jesus speaks of is because he knows that so many of us find that really difficult (and I include myself here). We don't always manage to love in the way that we are called to love. How often do we make God in our image and likeness?

Instead of worshipping the Holy Trinity of Father, Son and Spirit, we worship the Unholy Trinity of 'Me, Myself and I'. Is there something of which we need to let go?

Jesus' message is both radical and uncompromising. But it's also incredibly simple. It's a call to love. Jesus' love is a liberating love, a love that sets us free to know God as a loving parent. But this love is so often disrespected and minimised. How many times over the centuries have parents denied their children that freedom to love, when the person the child chooses to love is from the wrong family, the wrong side of town, or the person the child chooses to love has the wrong skin colour, is the wrong religion, the wrong gender or, heaven forbid, supports the wrong political party or the wrong football team?

If we truly want to be his disciples, then we have to be loving, compassionate, merciful and forgiving to all. And that includes those whom we find difficult to love, who sadly, can often be members of our own family, father against son, mother against daughter. It's a very tough message but one that plays out as different family members respond in their own way to the call of Christ and which ultimately divides a once cohesive group into something different. Different, not wrong. How willing are we to respect that?

Beyond our own families the challenge is still there. Can we love those who don't look or speak like we do? Can we love the disabled, the disfigured, the frail, the sick, the prisoner or the homeless? How willing are we to step away from what is deemed conventional to follow the footsteps of Jesus? Are we willing to make that sacrifice for the sake of the gospel? Only you will know the answer to that.

The good news is that we don't have to do all this on our own; that's where the baptism of fire comes in. Do we want this? Do we want this liberating love?

I know that in my own life I have told God many times that I do want to follow Jesus, to be his disciple. So often though, it's hard. It's hard to be the voice of peace. It's hard to go against the grain and to love and accept those whom society despises. It's hard to keep fighting for what you feel is right and good, when others don't see it the way you do. It's hard to refrain from judgement and condemnation.

If we do want more of God in our lives then the challenge for us is to let go, to let go of what binds and blinds us. The invitation is to surrender our egos to the gentle Spirit of God today and every day, to spend time in silence with Our Lord, saying nothing, doing nothing - simply let him do the work. That way, ultimately, as St Paul says, we will have the power to grasp the breadth and the length, the height and the depth until, knowing the love of Christ, which is beyond all knowledge, we will be filled with the utter fullness of God (Ephesians 3:18).

FOR PERSONAL REFLECTION

- Are you baptised? If so, in what ways are you living the life of a baptised Christian?
- Is there conflict in your life that needs God's healing?
- Are you ablaze with the Holy Spirit? If not, would you like to be?

WE PRAY

- that through the gift of our baptism, we will be bold and fearless in proclaiming our faith to those we meet
- for those we find difficult to love. Lord, help us to see them as you do
- for those areas of our life where we keep God out: Lord, help us to be open to your grace in all things
- for a greater understanding of the mission of Jesus, and the grace to follow him
- for all those areas of our lives, of our families and our world where there is conflict. Lord, help us to be beacons of your mercy and forgiveness.

Heavenly Father,
Thank you for the gift of your son Jesus and for the gift of the Holy Spirit. We pray that you will set our hearts on fire and keep them ablaze with your love. Help us to be faithful to you in all our thoughts, words and actions. We ask this through Christ our Lord.
Amen.

2. BE DRESSED AND READY

Jesus said to his disciples: 'See that you are dressed and ready for action and have your lamps lit. Be like men waiting for their master to return from the wedding feast, ready to open the door as soon as he comes and knocks. Happy those servants whom the master finds awake when he comes. I tell you solemnly, he will put on an apron, sit them down at table and wait on them. It may be in the second watch he comes, or in the third, but happy those servants if he finds them ready.'
(Luke 12:35-38)

REFLECTION

Have you ever had a job where you've had to be 'on call'? My husband was a police officer for 30 years and during that time he was often on call, particularly as he climbed the ladder of promotion. Others used to think it strange that he kept a pair of wellington boots, a warm coat, a torch, an A-Z road map and some yellow 'Police, do not cross' tape in the boot of his car.

The thing was though, that he was dressed and ready for action — prepared to preserve and deal with any scene of crime and I think that today's gospel is a spiritual version of being on call.

Jesus tells his disciples to be dressed, ready for action with lamps lit. What's he talking about? How do we dress ourselves, how do we keep our lamps blazing and what action does he mean?

I believe that Jesus is referring to ministry, both the ministry of his disciples and ours too. People often assume that ministry belongs exclusively to ordained clergy or those in religious life. Nothing could be further from the truth. We are all, by virtue of our baptism, called to minister in one way or another. Each of us has a unique calling. St Teresa of Calcutta once said: 'I can do things you cannot, you can do things I cannot; together we can do great things.'

Therefore, in order to be dressed and ready for action we need to know what action we're getting dressed for and when it will be needed.

How will we know this? I think it's useful to imagine what the servants are doing to prepare for the return of their master. First of all, they will need to know what is expected of them and what the master will want them to do when he does turn up.

In order to be dressed and ready for action, in order to know what the master will want, we need to spend time with God in prayer. How else will we know what it is that he expects us to do? How will we know what our unique ministry is?

When we spend time with God in the silence of our hearts, he will reveal to us the path he wishes us to take. If we are busy, forever rushing about and filling our lives with noise and chaos, how can we recognise that still small voice of our Creator? Remember that the words 'silent' and 'listen' are made up of the same letters. I believe that when Jesus exhorts us to be like servants waiting for the master to return, what he means is this: Pray, be still, find space and time for God in your lives, listen to his voice and wait.

That way, when God does come knocking you will know and recognise his voice and will find peace and consolation in it.

Being dressed, ready for action with our lamps lit means I think that in the life of every Christian, there will be multiple opportunities to witness to and live out our faith. We cannot do this unless we know what it is we believe and what it is we need to say or do. Spending time with God, reading the bible, becoming familiar and intimate with him, sharing our hopes and dreams and listening out for his voice in our lives will help us to do this.

In St Paul's letter to the Colossians (3:12) he writes, 'clothe yourselves with compassion, kindness, humility, gentleness and patience'.

In other words, it is our attitude towards others, our care for those who are in need, our love for all God's people, our generosity of heart and our ability to recognise the voice of God when he calls which will identify us as followers of Christ.

In this gospel reading the master of the house has gone away to a wedding feast and left the servants at home to keep the place in order. We may see this as the second coming of the Lord. We may even see it as pertaining to our own death, the time of which is known only to God. But for me, there are also two other messages in there.

First of all, look at the trust and the generosity of God. He's leaving us to care for this world he created, giving us both responsibility and free will. God's bounty is endless; everything we could possibly need or want is given to us through creation. This stunning planet of ours is rich in diversity and beauty.

Let's not forget however that we are, all of us, stewards of creation, accountable for the way we treat our home. When the master returns, what will he see? What will he find?

When Jesus says that the master may return in the second or third watch, I think this means that we cannot dictate God's timing. All that is required of us is to stay close to him and to trust that he knows what is best.

The second point is that there's also something here for me about the times in our lives when God seems absent – those times of spiritual dryness when we wonder where God's got to and what's keeping him. It can often feel that we're groping in the dark and there can be a real temptation to throw the God towel in, to tell him 'I'm not doing this anymore Lord; it's too hard'.

'How happy are those servants whose master finds them awake and ready'. In other words 'Keep going, don't give up. It will be worth it.'

What I love about this reading too is how Jesus regards service as something honourable, not lowly or demeaning. His rhetoric is so upside down and topsy turvy! There can be a tendency to see servants as rather unfortunate; minimum wage for waiters, carers and cleaners reflects that. But again, Jesus is out to restore the dignity of those whom we may judge as lowly. Whoever you are and whatever you do, know that you are relevant and important and you matter greatly to Our Lord, so much so that he will be so pleased to find you hard at work that he'll take over your job and wait on you! Just imagine that!

When Jesus tells his disciples that the master will sit them down at table and wait on them I believe that in these words what Jesus is asking us to do is to allow him to serve us, to get the Martha and Mary balance right. Sure it's good to serve Jesus when we look after others. However, the temptation can often be to rush around, keeping busy and ignoring God's voice. How many times did Our Lord go off to a lonely place to pray by himself, to be intimate with God? We all need this time of refreshment. We all need to hear that call of God, asking us to be still so that he can tell us just how beloved and precious we are to him. We need God to uphold and sustain us, especially when we are busy and occupied with his work. It's not wrong to sit in silence; on the contrary. To sit in stillness before God, even when it feels boring or pointless is, I believe, the singularly most important thing we can do each day. Because when we do, we will know when he comes knocking; we'll know his voice. Our lamps will be lit and we will be dressed and ready for action.

Know this too: by acknowledging that every time we go for reconciliation God is washing us clean. We light our lamps every time we read God's Holy Word and allow him to nourish our minds and hearts. Every time we receive Jesus in Holy Communion God is feeding and strengthening our bodies and our souls. Every moment we choose to spend with him God is allowing us to simply rest in his eternal love.

Jesus will come again. It may be in the second watch he comes, or in the third, but happy those servants if he finds them ready. The question is, are you ready?

To sum up then:
- This gospel is about being on call – waiting quietly so that we are ready to answer the call of God, whatever that may be.
- It's about God's trust in us and the responsibility we hold as stewards of creation.
- It's about the times when God seems absent and how he wants us to carry on anyway because it's important and worth it.
- Service is honourable, not demeaning, and there is joy to be had in it.
- Jesus will serve us too and each time we allow him to do that, we're better equipped for the work he wants us to do.

FOR PERSONAL REFLECTION
- Is there something in your spiritual dress code that marks you out as a Christian?
- How willing are you to spend time with God in silence so that you are ready when he calls?

- How much do you love God's creation?
- St Paul tells us to clothe ourselves with compassion, kindness, humility, gentleness and patience. Is there one of these things lacking in you? If so, do you need to bring this to God for healing?

WE PRAY
- for all those called to serve God in a special way, priests, deacons and religious. May they be strengthened and healed in their ministry
- for all believers, that through a life of prayer they will know when God comes knocking and be always ready to greet him
- for a greater respect for our planet. May we recognise the beauty and richness it offers and treat it with the love and care it deserves.

Loving and creator God,
Thank you for the gift of our faith. May we always treasure it and be willing to share it with others. Keep us awake, clothed in your love and with our lamps lit, ready to do your will. We ask this in total trust of your loving mercy.
Amen.

3. *WILL ONLY A FEW BE SAVED?*

Through towns and villages Jesus went teaching, making his way to Jerusalem. Someone said to him, 'Sir, will there be only a few saved?' He said to them, 'Strive to enter by the narrow gate, because, I tell you, many will try to enter and will not succeed.

'Once the master of the house has got up and locked the door, you may find yourself knocking on the door, saying, 'Lord, open to us' but he will answer, 'I do not know where you come from.' Then you will find yourself saying, 'We once ate and drank in your company; you taught in our streets' but he will reply, 'I do not know where you come from. Away from me, all you wicked men!'

'Then there will be weeping and grinding of teeth when you see Abraham and Isaac and Jacob and all the prophets in the East and West, from North and South, will come to take their places at the feast in the Kingdom of God.

'Yes, there are those now last who will be first, and those now first who will be last'.

(Luke 13:22-30)

REFLECTION
If Jesus were here, now, in the flesh, what would you ask him?

We are told in today's gospel that someone, we don't know who, asked him 'Sir, will only a few be saved?' I'm not sure that's the question I would have asked but when I read it, I recognise in the questioner something about myself. I believe that whoever asked that question had a bit of a subtext going on: Sir, will only a few be saved (and in brackets will I be one of them)? It's a yearning in all of us. Nobody wants to think of an after-life of misery and damnation. Therefore who would not want eternal life if it were offered?

Jesus is such a skilled teacher. He doesn't say 'yes', 'no' or 'don't ask silly questions'. What he does here is takes this seemingly peculiar question and turns it into a master class about the Kingdom of God – he is never off duty!

He begins by saying; 'Strive to enter by the narrow gate.' Such a strange answer! What does Jesus mean? The teaching goes that there is a gate in Jerusalem called 'The Eye of the Needle' through which a camel could not pass unless it had its baggage removed. After dark when the main gates were shut, travellers would have to use this smaller gate, through which the camel could only enter unencumbered and crawling on its knees. Jesus uses this strange metaphor to illustrate a deeper meaning.

Let me ask you this: what baggage do you need to shed in order to get through the narrow gate? Is there something that's blocking you from living the life God wants you to live? Maybe you're holding on to some resentment or hurt; this could be something that has happened so long ago that it would be too painful to revisit. I know from personal experience how emotionally difficult that can be. Perhaps you're resisting God's forgiveness and grace or allowing yourself to be lured by the earth's riches: maybe material possessions mean more to you than they should. Is now a good moment to approach God on your knees?

Alcoholics Anonymous (AA) runs a twelve step programme for recovery.

In Step 3 they are asked to turn their lives over to the care of God, *as they understand him*. I love this because it makes God big. So often we limit God's gifts by our perception of what we think we can handle. God is not some sugar-coated gentleman sitting on a cloud, nor is he some vengeful, exacting demon. This loving God is infinitely greater than anything we could ever imagine. God wants to take from us everything that might prevent us from entering by the narrow gate, from knowing exactly who he is.

In Step 4 AA members make a searching and fearless moral inventory of themselves and in Step 7 they humbly ask God to remove their shortcomings – a bit like the sacrament of reconciliation. I find this type of surrender a beautiful and very practical way of striving to enter by the narrow gate – the gate that leads to freedom.

Allow me to use this analogy to demonstrate what I mean. When I can, I cycle along the River Mersey in Stockport where the path that I use has gates along it to stop motorbikes from getting through. It's a real inconvenience for me to have to keep getting off my bike to get through these gaps. But the thing is that if I didn't get off, I would be missing out. Because beyond each gate is more beauty for me to enjoy. If I just turned round and went back the way I'd come, I'd only see that one small section of the river. I'd be missing out on the vast and infinite wonder of God's creation, the ever changing colours, textures, sounds and sights that are on offer. And so by squeezing through the gap with my bike I'm gaining – not losing. And so it is with God: each time we shed something that keeps us from him, we gain even more than we already had.

Passing through these narrow gates causes me to slow down. When we seek the forgiveness of God in the sacrament of reconciliation we too slow down to reflect. Sin encumbers us; it ties us down and slows us down. But then coming out can feel like a huge gate has been flung open; we see the contrast of being weighed down by sin and then set free.

The narrow gate has another meaning – that is, you have to pass through it alone. You cannot go through a turnstile side by side with another person. For me that symbolises the unique calling of each of us. I cannot do what you do and you cannot do what I do. I can lead and I can follow but ultimately I can only enter eternity by myself. Each of us makes that final journey alone.

The second half of this reading tells us just that. We should try to seize the opportunities that we're offered in this life before it's too late. Jesus warns us about knocking on the door after the master has closed it; that we may call out for the door to be opened because we once ate and drank in his company.

We can eat and drink in the company of others and have no level of intimacy whatsoever with them. We could come to church and do good deeds but Jesus wants and calls us to be so intimate with him that we come to know him as much as he knows us. Jesus came to show us the love of God the Father. Why wouldn't he want that relationship with us when he's gone to the painstaking trouble of counting every hair on our head and making sure that no two people in the whole world have the same fingerprints? But we cannot be close and personal unless we shake off the stuff that prevents us from being that way with him. That's the price we pay for discipleship.

How do we do this? I believe that the answer is in silent prayer, in bringing ourselves before God and allowing him to do the work. Maybe you could try taking some time each day to sit in stillness before the one who made you. Ask him to reveal to you anything that prevents you from knowing who God is - the one who loved you into being and who will love you into eternity.

As I write this piece, we are in the middle of the Coronavirus pandemic. I don't know about you but over the months I have come to realise that so little is truly necessary, that I can live far more simply than I have been doing. The one certainty has been God whose love and presence is steadfast and true. For me this has been a time to take stock and to see what I can manage without. Treading lightly feels so much better. My prayer is that each of us can learn about what really matters: love, service, community, connection, kindness, generosity of spirit, selflessness and a commitment to take better care of our planet.

Abraham, Isaac and Jacob knew that, as did all the saints who have gone ahead of us into glory. Through the difficulties of

life, each of them found God in the silence of their hearts. All of
them in their struggles found the strength to let God be God.
The more we read about the lives of the prophets and saints, the
more we realise that they were as flawed and broken as we are.
But we can still listen to them, learn from them and ask for their
guidance and intercession. We cannot inherit eternal life by our
own strength. We simply have to ask Jesus to remove whatever
it is that's blocking our path to freedom – after all, he is the gate
to salvation.

Finally, there is one word in that text that speaks volumes to me
– it's the word 'strive'.

Jesus does not say 'You must', 'you should', 'you've got to',
'you've got no chance unless'. No, he says 'strive' - try your best.
I believe that it says everything about God's loving, tender
mercy and compassion. He knows we're imperfect but loves us
anyway and never stops reaching out to offer us that
unconditional love. Let's pray for the grace to accept and
embrace it, even when we mess up.

FOR PERSONAL REFLECTION
- What does the narrow gate mean to you?
- Is there something preventing you from going into a
  deeper relationship with God? If so, can you ask him
  to take it from you?
- Are you fearful that somebody you love may not be
  saved? If so, can you give this fear to God?

WE PRAY

- for the times we have ignored the narrow gate of discipleship and taken the wide road of selfishness, greed, resentment and anger. Forgive us Lord
- that we may always be open and willing to learn from Jesus, even when it's difficult
- for all those who don't know God, those who are searching for purpose and meaning in their lives and those who have known him but have rejected his love.

Loving Jesus,
You are the narrow gate that leads to freedom. You are the way to salvation. Give us the grace to follow you closely, even when it seems impossible, and to trust in your great love and mercy.
Amen.

PART TWO

AUTHORITY AND CHOICE

4. *GOD SO LOVED THE WORLD*
For God so loved the world that he gave his only Son, so that every-one who believes in him might not perish but might have eternal life. For God did not send his Son into the world to condemn the world, but that through him the world might be saved. Whoever believes in him will not be condemned, but whoever does not believe has already been condemned, because he has not believed in the name of the only Son of God. And this is the verdict, that the light came into the world, but people preferred darkness to light, because their works were evil. For everyone who does wicked things hates the light and does not come toward the light, so that his works might not be exposed. But whoever lives the truth comes to the light, so that his works may be clearly seen as done in God.
(John 3: 16-21)

REFLECTION
To begin this reflection I have two questions for you to consider:

 1. How would you feel if I asked you to give away your most treasured possession?
 2. How you would feel if you were asked to tell a group of people the worst thing you have ever done?

Please bear with me – both questions are relevant.

24

God loved the world so much that he gave his only Son. A child is the most precious thing any parent could want. I have heard many parents talking about the difficulties they face when their children leave home; some call it 'empty nest syndrome'. And whilst every parent knows it has to happen, it comes at a great emotional price. Any love is a costly commodity, especially parental love. I have heard many parents say that they would give anything to ensure that their child was safe and happy.

God gave the world his most treasured possession – not a piece of jewellery, a family heirloom, a car or a house; he gave the world his only Son. He did this in full knowledge of the itinerant life Jesus would live, the rejection he would experience and ultimately the ignominious death he would suffer. But he did it anyway. God made that ultimate sacrifice. That is how much he loves you and me. And I believe too that if you were the only person on earth, God would have sent his Son to die just for you.

I think it's also worth noting the words, 'For God so loved the world'. John's gospel doesn't say, 'For the world so loved God'. Jesus is not a gift that we have somehow deserved or merited because of the way we love or serve our creator. Jesus is the most precious gift we could ever want, given freely without conditions or restraint by the one who loved us first and the one who will love us into eternity. That is the supreme, utmost generosity and bounteousness of God. No matter who we are, what our social standing is, what our history or background is, God loves us.

God gave us the gift of Jesus so that we would not be lost. Again and again in the gospels we read stories of how Jesus sought out the lost: the parable of the missing sheep, the lost coin, the Samaritan woman at the well, the woman who touched his cloak, the woman caught committing adultery, Mary of Magdala, Levi, Zacchaeus, Bartimeus; the list goes on.

What does it mean to be lost? Lost in what? Being lost means we can't find our way somewhere. People can be lost in loneliness and isolation, in bad relationships, in spiritual blindness, in despair or in a cycle of sin. People can be lost when they don't feel needed. In my counselling work, I have come across many children who are lost through feelings of inadequacy. 'I'm not attractive enough, clever enough, popular enough, likeable enough.'

Each one of them, without fail, has been lost in some way, looking for an escape from sadness and feelings of insufficiency.

God doesn't want that. He wants us to know where we are going, to be certain of our destination and of how to get there – to Zion, the Holy City of God. You and I are heaven bound, where one day we will see God face to face. Nobody said the journey would be easy – there may be so many obstacles which mean we have to go back and start down a different path. But God keeps on beckoning us towards him, with the Holy Spirit to guide us.

But, you know, the everlasting or eternal life Jesus speaks of in this passage is not just something for after we die. It starts now, in this moment, in the life of our eternal God which flows in us and through us. This life is free, free of charge. We don't have to DO anything to get it – Jesus did that bit already. We just have to accept it.

Writer and speaker Frances Hogan, in her reflections on St Paul's ministry, once said that she would need the whole of eternity just to thank God for what he has already done for her in this life. It may be worth thinking about this, about the gifts which God pours into your lap, day after day. Sometimes the temptation is to turn to God when we are desperate or in need; other times it's to complain to him about things that may be going wrong for us. How often do we turn to God in simple gratitude for the air that we breathe, for the food on our table, for the kindness of others, for the love we share and for the gift of Jesus? Are we aware that every time we open our eyes from sleep, that each new day is a gift from God?

There's a tough message too though in this bit of John's gospel. Jesus says that he's not come to condemn the world but that whoever refuses to believe is condemned already. So if Jesus hasn't come to condemn the world, then who is doing the condemning?

I have counselled people who suffer from alcohol or drug addiction. A good number of those with whom I have worked have been brought up in Christian households. I have listened to many clients talk about the guilt and shame around their behaviour and from the choices they've made. What makes me feel really sad is that the God they understand is often a God of judgement and harshness. The condemnation they feel is not from a loving Creator but from someone else's negative view of God, passed onto them in childhood.

We cannot live in the light if we refuse to acknowledge God's mercy for everybody. We cannot live in the light when we reject God's saving power for everybody. God loves us in our goodness and in our sinfulness; condemnation comes only when we fail to see that God loves us all, no matter who we are or what we have done.

When we refuse to believe, we are condemned already. Maybe what Jesus is saying here is that his grace is for everyone. Refusing to believe that we can be recipients of it will condemn us to a life of misunderstanding, of not knowing who we are in the eyes of our beautiful Creator. Each of us is a beloved child of God, a God who causes the sun to shine on the righteous and the unrighteous alike (Matthew 5:45). Living without this knowledge is, I believe, what Jesus meant. When we reject or minimise or diminish the unconditional love of God, we're not free. We're bound by the chains of misunderstanding, of boxing God off, of making him in our image and likeness. Can we ask God to break those chains?

We cannot live in the light unless we too know God's mercy. Sadly, there is a familiarity, a safety and anonymity in the darkness – and in the protective wall that keeps us there.

There is always a choice; we can choose to trust, to surrender, to believe and to receive God's grace or we can choose not to.

WE complicate it, not God. We make God so small. Too often we can't accept that God loves us because we don't really love ourselves. I think we're all frightened of being shown up as evil and guilty. I asked you at the start how you would feel about sharing the worst thing you'd ever done in front of a group of people. We don't want those things brought into the light when they are shameful or embarrassing. We may feel rejected if people knew what we were really like.

To get back to the people with whom I work... when I listen to their stories, I often feel as though I'm sitting in the heart of God himself and, in some small way, I can see them through the eyes of Jesus. This is my Holy Ground. I know that it's a gift, but I see that as part of the eternal life that Jesus offers to all of us, not just to me. St Teresa of Calcutta once said that if you judge people, you have no time to love them. When we condemn others and when we condemn ourselves, then we can never be free. The light of God's love will never hurt our eyes – it just shows us the way to salvation.

We can only truly discover that God loves us just as we are when we accept the fact that we are all broken and poor before him. None of us is perfect. God does not demand that we are attractive, clever, popular or likeable; God does not demand that we are successful, nor does he demand that we do everything well. It is only when we know this at the deepest level of our being that we can live in the truth and the light of our Heavenly Father.

Jesus' death took place to show us that there are no barriers to God's love, a love that is for everyone. There is no greater love than this (John 5:13).

God loved the world so much that He gave His only Son, so that everyone who believes in Him may not be lost, but may have eternal life.

FOR PERSONAL REFLECTION
- Are you lost in some way or other? Can you ask God to help you?
- God loves you, just as you are. Do you know this?

WE PRAY
- for those who find it difficult to believe in a God who loves them
- for all who feel lost in the darkness of sin
- for those who struggle with addiction
- for those who judge and condemn others.

Loving God,
You generously offered to the world your son Jesus. Thank for this precious gift. Help us to know him better and to serve him faithfully. Amen.

5. JESUS TEACHES FROM A BOAT ON A LAKE

Jesus withdrew with his disciples to the lakeside, and great crowds from Galilee followed him. From Judaea, Jerusalem, Idumaea, Transjordania and the region of Tyre and Sidon, great numbers who had heard of all he was doing came to him. And he asked his disciples to have a boat ready for him because of the crowd, to keep him from being crushed. For he had cured so many, that all who were afflicted in any way were crowding forward to touch him. And the unclean spirits, whenever they saw him, would fall down before him and shout 'You are the Son of God!' But he warned them strongly not to make him known.
(Mark 3: 7-12)

REFLECTION

Have you ever had one of those weeks when everything you do is met with disapproval or criticism? In this gospel Jesus has just had one of those weeks. Prior to this incident in Chapter 2 of Mark's gospel he was criticised for telling a paralysed man that his sins were forgiven (Mark 2:6), censured for eating with sinners (Mark 2:16), condemned because John's disciples fasted but his didn't (Mark 2:18). The scribes and Pharisees questioned why Jesus' disciples were picking ears of corn on the Sabbath (Mark 2:24); how dare they succumb to that basic instinct of physical hunger? Finally Jesus is watched closely and accused of breaking the Sabbath again as he heals a man with a withered hand (Mark 3:16).

No wonder Jesus headed off for the lake! There's a song by the

Irish folk singer Christie Moore called 'Lisdoonvarna' in which he says 'Everybody needs a break, climb a mountain, jump in a lake'. For me a lake symbolises both tranquillity and power, healing and cleansing and, whether you immerse yourself in the water or sit on the shore and look at it, water has that ability to restore us, to make us feel better and calmer.

We have to remember that Jesus came to earth as fully divine and fully human and, at the start of this story, we see again the humanity of the Lord. He's probably fed up of being criticised, he's tired and in need of a rest. There is no human emotion that we can ever feel that Christ hasn't felt already and I find that comforting because it helps me to see that Jesus is my friend, my confidant, my brother, my counsellor and my advocate with the Father.

Jesus, we read, takes his disciples with him on this occasion. I think he has two reasons for doing this. First of all, when we are feeling low we sometimes need to spend time with our friends who will reassure and validate us, who will make us laugh, help us to forget our problems for a while or put things into perspective. And maybe Jesus needed that. The second reason is that he was about to choose his 12 apostles. So maybe this was a testing time for them. He needed to know that they would be able to handle the itinerant, almost nomadic lifestyle that he was offering. Could they cope with the great crowds of people surrounding Jesus? Could they really give up everything to follow him?

In this gospel, Mark is at great pains to tell us all the different places the people travelled from to meet Christ. Why does he do that? For two reasons I believe.

First of all, it's to show us that Jesus' love, healing and compassion is for everybody. Age, origin, skin colour, gender, social standing, employment, marital status and finances are of no importance to Our Lord. His love encompasses the whole of humanity – no exceptions. God can use anybody at any hour and in any place, no matter who you are or what your history is. His love transcends all the limitations we put on others. Nobody is insignificant to our Heavenly Father.

I also believe that Mark does this to tell us that every encounter with Christ involves a journey. Our journey of faith can be smooth or rocky, straight or bendy, high or low. There may be obstacles of all shapes and sizes. Metaphorically we may get burnt by the sun, blown over by the wind, soaked by the rain but ultimately it's always worth it. Jesus knows the trouble to which we have gone to reach him and that's why he never turns us away. And sometimes, when we get there, we are so exhausted that all we can do is collapse at his feet and allow him to lift us up, anoint our sores, bind our wounds, restore and refresh us. We are all afflicted and we all need to touch Jesus. Every person who made that journey to be at the lakeside that day had, I believe, a divine appointment with Christ. And I can't help thinking too that each individual who encountered the Lord went away different – like the Wise Men and the shepherds, touched, healed, transformed. How could they not be?

But we hear that the crowds were so huge that they were almost crushing him in their bid to get close. He had cured so many who were afflicted in any way. Who were these troubled individuals? Maybe among them were lepers, the blind, the deaf, the lame, those with mental health problems, those wounded from abuse and violence, the disfigured, the outcasts – all welcomed without judgement as precious children of God. Jesus offers so much more than a physical healing. He is concerned too with our hearts and our souls. He sees there in that crowd the desperation, the hope, the desire for change.

So Jesus asks his disciples to get a boat ready for him. This makes me smile; imagine Jesus saying 'Do you know what? I'm feeling a bit claustrophobic here with this lot. Could you just sort me out a boat?' What did they imagine he was going to do?

But it's Jesus' absolute authority that gets me. Most people giving a talk would usually stand up and use a microphone to address the audience; often that would take place in a covered building. There was Jesus, out on the lake with the crowds around him, maybe babies crying or dogs barking, the sound of the waves and the other fishing boats going about their business. And he has the courage, the ultimate charisma and the supreme authority to speak to them sitting in a boat!

What did Jesus say? Mark doesn't give us this information; he is more concerned with showing us that the Kingdom of God manifests itself in the healings of Christ, that his authority is proved by his actions rather than his words. God's Kingdom is about real life; it is not something reserved for death; it's here and it's now. Jesus shows us that in the ordinariness of our lives, God's power can break through to bring about deep healing and mercy -- but only when we seek Christ in sincerity and truth.

Nevertheless, I believe that Jesus' message is always very simple. He is their journey's end. He came that they and we may have life and have it to the full. Jesus is the Way, the Truth, the Life, the Alpha and the Omega. He came to bring the good news to the poor, to set prisoners free; he is God's holy anointed one, the Messiah, the fulfilment of God's promise. This message is for you and me too in this very moment and in every moment of our lives.

At the end of the story we hear Jesus telling the unclean spirits not to make him known. Why did Mark include this short verse?

This warning not to tell anyone is a literary technique that Mark uses called the 'Messianic Secret' and it is there because he wants us to experience Jesus for ourselves and not rely on what others tell us. Mark has already told us who Jesus is in the first line of his Gospel when he writes, 'This is the Good News about Jesus Christ, the Son of God.' (Mark 1:1) So maybe here Jesus wanted the crowd to come to their own conclusion about him by what they saw, heard and experienced, rather than have evil spirits point it out to them.

Perhaps too, Jesus doesn't want his message to be affected or blurred by an unclean source. I know for some people faith can be seen almost like a superstition, more of a duty than a living relationship. I don't think Jesus wants this. I think he wants to set us free from anything that ties us down and prevents us from knowing that we're loved anyway – regardless of what we do. We have no need to appease a God who loves us implicitly and unconditionally.

I believe that this short passage tells us so much of both the humanity and the divinity of Christ. On a human level it speaks of his need to get away, to be with friends, to rest and recuperate. However, it speaks too of his command over sickness and disease, his gentle teaching and his supreme power over the Evil One.

Not only that, but I think this account gently invites us to carve out time to be with Jesus in the lake of our minds and to listen to his voice, speaking directly to our hearts so that we hear his message with clarity and openness.

FOR PERSONAL REFLECTION
- Can you trust Jesus with all your emotions, positive and negative, knowing that he has felt them too?
- Do you know that Jesus is your journey's beginning and end, the Alpha and the Omega?
- Can you make time in your day to recognise the call of Christ, to deepen your relationship by creating opportunities to be alone with him?

WE PRAY
- for all those who are making that journey into the heart of God, those whose faith is being tested or those who have given up trying. Help them Lord, to recognise that you are their journey's end
- for those who are struggling to recognise the presence of Christ in their lives. Give us the strength to make you known through our witness
- for refugees, especially those who make the perilous journey across the sea to look for freedom and security
- for those who feel under spiritual attack of any sort. Help them to know your loving presence in their lives.

Loving Jesus,
You sat in a boat to teach us the way to salvation. Help us to listen to your words which bring life and freedom. Help us to understand that to you nothing is impossible and to know in the depths of our hearts that you alone are the fulfilment of all our desires.
Amen.

6. PICK UP YOUR STRETCHER

Jesus was teaching one day, and among the audience there were Pharisees and doctors of the law who had come from Galilee, from Judea and from Jerusalem. And the power of the Lord was behind his works of healing. Then some men appeared, carrying on a bed a paralysed man whom they were trying to bring in and lay down in front of him. But as the crowd made it impossible to find a way of getting him in, they went up onto the flat roof and lowered him and his stretcher down through the tiles into the middle of the gathering, in front of Jesus. Seeing their faith he said, 'My friend, your sins are forgiven you.'

The scribes and the Pharisees began to think this over, 'Who is this man talking blasphemy? Who can forgive sins but God alone?' But Jesus, aware of their thoughts, made them this reply, 'Why are you thinking these things in your hearts? Which of these is easier to say, 'Your sins are forgiven you,' or to say, 'Get up and walk'? But to prove to you that the Son of Man has authority on earth to forgive sins,' - he said to the paralysed man, 'I order you: get up, and pick up your stretcher and go home.' And immediately before their very eyes, he got up, picked up what he had been lying on and went home praising God.
They were all astounded and praised God, and were filled with awe, saying, 'We have seen strange things today.'
(Luke 5:17-25)

REFLECTION

Whoever said the bible was boring? I find this story very funny. The idea of lowering a man on a stretcher through the roof of a building is ludicrous and outlandish. With every gospel story though, we have to look for the deeper meaning of who we believe Jesus to be and what it means to follow him.

To help us delve into these questions, I'd like to take this story literally and to see what deeper levels of understanding Luke might want us to gain from it.

Jesus once said that unless we become like little children, we cannot enter the Kingdom of God (Matthew 18:3). Children ask many questions, relentlessly (and sometimes annoyingly). When reading the gospels, I find it useful to approach them with an enquiring mind. This helps me to see how relevant these accounts are today and how God's power can and does break through, when we live in expectant hope.

Here we find Jesus teaching in a house packed full of people. They had come from all over the land, leading members of the faith among them, to hear what Jesus had to say. From every village they had come. Why? What was it about Christ that drew so many to him? Luke doesn't tell us what Jesus was saying, only that the power of the Lord was with him.

Imagine that for a moment. The gospels are littered with examples of Jesus' supreme authority over infirmity and death. Luke's focus here was not on his words, but on his divinity. The power of the Lord was with him.

I wonder how many in the crowd recognised that. How many listening and watching knew that here in their midst was the

Holy One of God? Whose eyes do we have when we think about Jesus - those of the Pharisees or those of the crippled man? Can we see Christ around us? Do you know that in your everyday life, in every encounter you have with another person, the Holy One of God is there, dwelling within each of us?

Meanwhile some men were carrying to Christ a paralytic on a stretcher.

I love this.

How many men? Did they take turns holding the corners? How far had they come? Why were they late?

I don't know about you, but I have been carried on a stretcher during some fitness training classes. It was a singularly uncomfortable experience and one I would not wish to repeat. Carrying it was no better.

Here were these men bringing another man to Christ. Why was he on a stretcher? Had he been crippled from birth or in an accident? Whatever the reason, life would have been tough, with condemnation over him for having sinned himself or for having ancestors who had displeased God. This man would have been rejected or scorned and unwelcome in polite society, . However, we know that Jesus' love was always a preferential love for those whom society belittled. His love was and still is all-embracing; nobody is outside the circle of Christ's acceptance, nobody. No matter who you are or what your history is, God loves you.

As I said, we don't know this man's background or even his name. The gospels often leave out these details, inviting us to delve deeper so that we can examine our own attitudes to others. Do we ever stop to consider what life is like for our neighbours? Do we ever pause to think about ways in which we can alleviate the suffering of those around us? Can we carry that stretcher to Christ in our prayers and in our service?

We don't know if this man had a family to support. Again, the details are omitted so that we can deepen our empathy and appreciation for the poor, the sick and the disabled in our own midst.

What I don't get is why these men came late. Had they known there was going to be a crowd? If so, why not set off earlier? I like to imagine simple reasons for this: oversleeping, a hangover maybe, a row, returning for the forgotten packed lunch, stopping for comfort breaks or to swap sides with the stretcher. These are all human experiences speaking to us through time and space. You see, when things don't go according to plan, maybe it's because there is a greater plan. All we are ever called to be is faithful to the process and to allow the Holy Spirit to work out the meaning of that plan in our lives. There is always a Plan B when God is involved!

Imagine these men arriving and seeing the crowds. They'd come all that way to meet the Lord. They were probably hot, sweaty, thirsty, grumpy maybe and sore from the carrying. Does that deter them? Absolutely not!

In this part of the gospel account, we are being taught a very valuable and significant lesson. It is this: believe the impossible, no matter how impossible it may seem.

Faith in God doesn't mean that everything will be handed to us on a plate or that life will be without difficulties. Faith does not exempt us from challenges and trials. On the contrary, faith presents us with many complications and problems but, at the same time, invites us to trust in a God who loves us, who wants only what is best for us, who wants to shower us with his blessings and who calls us into an ever-deeper relationship with him. Faith challenges us to let go of all that binds us and to see that in the complexities of life, our loving Creator is always there to provide solace, strength, courage and hope. Faith asks us to believe at the deepest level of our being that God alone is enough.

I love the outrageous audacity of these men and the compassion they show to their paralysed friend. Regardless of the obstacles, they formed a plan. Undaunted they carried it through, remaining faithful and committed. What a wonderful example of friendship and discipleship! To take a stretcher onto a roof requires skill and courage. To remove the roof tiles of someone else's home is utterly preposterous. I also think it's absolutely hilarious. I have this image of Jesus in a dark room, surrounded by bodies. Gradually the room gets lighter. The sun comes in. Maybe dust, debris and bits of roof start dropping into the hair of those present. I like to see this scene in my mind's eye, of eyes looking up in astonishment, of minds collectively thinking, 'What the blazes is going on?'

I love too how the men lower the stretcher, putting their friend's needs first and allowing him to meet the Lord just as he is. This is so important, because that is exactly how Jesus wants us to meet him, just as we are. We don't need to wait until we've got our lives sorted to come before God. We are not required to be in a calm and loving state of mind in order to encounter the Lord. No. We come just as we are, angry, hurt or afraid, at peace, at war, in bitterness, in sorrow, in resentment, in harmony. It matters not to God. We are simply invited to turn up.

What I also love about this story is how the man doesn't speak. Words can often be highly overrated, particularly when it comes to prayer. Silence is a powerful way of allowing God to be God.

And here, Jesus proves exactly that. 'Your sins are forgiven,' he says. Only God has the authority to forgive sins. Here Luke wants us to know exactly who Jesus is, the Son of God.

Instead of rejoicing over the healing of this man, the Pharisees are angry. Their silence is not a loving one, but one that is full of outrage. How can this man commit such blasphemy? Their blindness is both disappointing but human, born of jealousy and misunderstanding. But look how Jesus meets them where they are, explaining and rephrasing without backing down. Luke wants us to see the deific authority of Christ. Only God has the power to forgive sins. Jesus is part of that Godhead, fully human and fully divine.

Why else does Jesus use these words? It's because he is far more concerned with the heart than with how we look. By centering on 'pick up your stretcher', that would bring it to the physical and the visual. In other words, Jesus would be focusing merely on what others can see. Christ wants to heal the soul; the words he uses reflect that. Jesus wants to focus on those unseen parts of us, the deeper facets of our being. It's not about appearance – it's about depth and heart, about knowing who we are in the sight of God – his Beloved.

Whatever the words, the outcome is the same. This man is cured, healed and set free. Jesus' healing power does not stop here. Can we claim this for ourselves?

FOR PERSONAL REFLECTION
- Who do we bring to Christ?
- How do we treat the disabled in our midst?
- Can we come to Jesus just as we are and allow him to heal us?

WE PRAY
- for the disabled of mind and body
- for those entrusted with care of the sick
- for those on the journey of faith.

Lord, I believe. Help my unbelief. Lord, increase my faith. Amen.

7. *A VOICE WAS HEARD IN RAMAH*

After the Wise Men had left, the angel of the Lord appeared to Joseph in a dream and said, 'Get up, take the child and his mother with you, and escape into Egypt, and stay there until I tell you, because Herod intends to search for the child and do away with him.' So Joseph got up and, taking the child and his mother with him, left that night for Egypt, where he stayed until Herod was dead. This was to fulfil what the Lord had spoken through the prophet:

I called my son out of Egypt.

Herod was furious when he realised that he had been outwitted by the Wise Men and in Bethlehem and its surrounding district he had all the male children killed who were two years old or under, reckoning by the date he had been careful to ask the wise men. It was then that the words spoken through the prophet Jeremiah were fulfilled:

A voice was heard in Ramah,
Sobbing and loudly lamenting:
It was Rachel weeping for her children,
Refusing to be comforted,
Because they were no more.
(Matthew 2: 13-18)

REFLECTION

Maybe like me you find this reading very disturbing, particularly after the joy of Christmas. It is for us a stark reminder of the forces of evil at work in our world and that we cannot remain in the stable at Bethlehem. Discipleship is not about keeping the baby Jesus in the manger; rather it is about bringing him into the world, into our lives, our struggles, our hopes and our desires. And, with every gospel reading, we need to see what it is telling us about our lives today.

There is however, one word that sums up this reading for me – it's the word 'fear'. It seems that everyone is afraid and no one more so than Herod himself.

The famous psychiatrist Elisabeth Kübler Ross once said that there are two basic motivating forces, fear and love. All other emotions are sub-categories of these two.

In Herod we see fear at its most menacing. What level of insecurity must he have suffered to feel so threatened by a baby? We know from his dialogue with the Wise Men that the seed of revenge had already been planted. 'When you find him, let me know, so that I too may go and pay him homage' (Matthew 2:8). Lies – pure lies! Herod had no intention of paying homage to anything other than his own ego. He worshipped not the Holy Trinity of Father, Son and Spirit, rather that Unholy Trinity of Me, Myself and I.

What offends me more than anything else in this story is that he gave orders to have these baby boys killed, rather than kill them himself. He took the coward's way out. How long did it take him to come to that appalling decision? How much time did he spend pondering his options? Who, if anybody, advised him? Were his advisers scared too? Were they afraid for their positions, their status, their families? Did anybody challenge this unspeakable verdict? If so what was the outcome? And what was Herod doing whilst this cruel massacre was taking place? Eating, drinking, sleeping, carrying on as normal? Fear can paralyse us into doing nothing or into going along with what we know in our hearts to be wrong. It is a very human response, to turn a blind eye, to fail to act in the face of injustice when it is played out before our very eyes.

When we look at the life of Jesus, we see such a contrast. He used his authority to heal, to welcome the outcasts, to raise the dignity of those bowed down, to liberate and to love.

And what of the men who carried out these killings? How did they feel, charging through the villages on horseback, with murder on their minds? I think they too were afraid; we can be afraid of appearing weak amongst our peers, afraid to stand up for what is right and just. How did they feel pushing a screaming mother out of the way while they murdered her child? Were any of them obliged to kill one of their own children in accordance with this edict? Were their hearts so coarsened that they were able to sleep peacefully at night with no flashbacks or nightmares? Somehow I doubt it.

And the parents, siblings and families – what of them? Not only would some of them have been forced to watch them being murdered but some would have faced an appalling choice. Because if the parents had tried to protect their baby, they too could be killed and then what would happen to their other children? Would they have been left orphans? Would it have been easier to simply hand the baby over to death than to leave the others without anyone to look after them? It's an unimaginable dilemma.

How does a family, a community, a country deal with the aftermath of that horror? No wonder a voice is heard in Ramah. No wonder there is weeping and great mourning; Rachel weeping for her children and refusing to be comforted, because they are no more (Jeremiah 31:15). Rachel represents all those who, in the course of history, mourn the loss of innocence, the blameless victims of violence, war, genocide, abortion, grooming and abuse.

We can think of killings on a global mass scale in our recent history but the abuse and violence continues in our own communities, anywhere where the dignity and protection of human life are disrespected.

What really saddens me is that if Herod had gone to pay homage to the Infant King of the Jews then none of this would have happened. Because when we gaze at Jesus and he gazes at us, fear is replaced by love. Jesus is no threat. In him we find our greatest treasure – that of knowing that we are God's beloved sons and daughters. He will never abandon us or forsake us. Our names are written in his book.

Joseph knew that. At the beginning of this gospel we read that the angel visited him again, this time telling him to take Mary and Jesus down to Egypt. Joseph has already been told once by the angel not to be afraid. 'Don't be afraid to take Mary home as your wife' (Matthew 1:20). Once again he obeys instantly, leaving for Egypt that night; he leaves everything behind. He is a perfect example of discipleship.

I am a trained linguist and I used to work for Greater Manchester Police, interpreting for complainants or those in custody who were unable to communicate in English. On one particular occasion I was asked to help a French speaking Congolese asylum seeker. Her story was horrific: she had suffered unimaginable abuse in her native country until one day she had seen an opportunity to escape and taken it. She left her family, her friends, her community and her country to arrive here on foreign soil with nothing other than the clothes on her back. Her name was Carol and she was just 19 years old.

What did Joseph leave behind? Was he able to tell anyone they were leaving or did they simply disappear? He and Mary would have had to leave their home, their possessions, their families, their source of emotional and practical support, Joseph's work and income.

What did he face in this new land? Were they welcome? Did they have to learn a new language or dialect? Did he find work? Were he and Mary homesick? I'm sure they were. The gospels are full of life, of everyday circumstances and dilemmas, of thoughts and feelings which speak to us down the centuries – always with a challenge. Who said the bible was irrelevant?

There is such a contrast between Herod and Joseph:

Herod cannot trust in God's providence. Joseph does.

Herod is motivated by power. Joseph has no motivation other than to carry out God's will.

Herod is life destroying. Joseph is life saving.

Herod succumbs to his fears. Joseph overcomes his fears.

Herod is reactive. Joseph is proactive.

Herod cannot look at Jesus. Joseph can.

Herod's actions were wicked. Joseph's were only good.

Herod personifies fear. Joseph personifies love.

Because where there is love, we can find peace, acceptance, serenity and trust. Where there is fear we find discomfort, anger, aggression, blame and revenge. You see, when love overwhelms, fear cannot surface, and where fear overwhelms, love cannot surface. We, each of us, have a choice, to live in love or to live in fear.

The Holy Innocents are few, in comparison to the mass slaughter of innocents throughout history. Nevertheless, even if there had been only one Holy Innocent, we recognise the greatest treasure God put on the earth – a human person, destined for eternity and graced by Jesus, the infant babe in the manger.

Let me leave you with this reflection based on the words of Isaiah 43:1.

Every morning we need to whisper this message to our anxious hearts:

Do not be afraid for I have redeemed you. I have called you by your name. You are mine. When you take on the swirling rapids, as I hope you will, you will not drown. When you walk through the leaping flames, as one day you must, you will not be harmed. You are the apple of my eye. You are so very precious in my sight. I have carved your name in the palm of my hand. Your name is 'My Delight, My Beloved, My Betrothed.' Amen.
(Source anon)

FOR PERSONAL REFLECTION
- By what do we feel threatened? Can we ask for the grace to let go of that fear?
- Do we seek revenge for those who have hurt us? Can we ask for God's healing touch on our pain?
- Have we stood by in the face of injustice? Do we need God's forgiveness?
- Can we allow love to be the motivating factor of our lives?

WE PRAY
- for children everywhere, especially the victims of war, abuse and cruelty
- for all families who have lost a child, especially those whose death is a result of violence
- for parents, teachers, childminders and all those entrusted with the care of little ones

- for all those who are afraid, whose lives are full of insecurity and anxiety, for those who battle mental illness and addiction. We ask God to shine his light of love into the darkness of their fear
- for all those who are guilty of murder. May they know the forgiving love of Christ.

Loving and Creator God,
You hold our fragile world in the palm of your ever loving hands. Please hear our prayers which we make in total trust of your loving mercy. Through Christ our Lord.
Amen.

8. JESUS ENCOUNTERS A ROMAN CENTURION

When Jesus went into Capernaum, a centurion came up and pleaded with him. 'Sir,' he said, 'my servant is lying at home paralysed, and in great pain.' 'I will come myself and cure him,' said Jesus. The centurion replied, 'Sir, I am not worthy to have you under my roof; just give the word and my servant will be cured. For I am under authority myself, and have soldiers under me; and I say to one man: Go, and he goes; to another: Come here, and he comes; to my servant: Do this, and he does it.' When Jesus heard this he was astonished and said to those following him, 'I tell you solemnly, nowhere in Israel have I found faith like this. And I tell you that many will come from East and West to take their places with Abraham and Isaac and Jacob at the feast in the Kingdom of heaven; but the subjects of the Kingdom will be turned out into the dark, where there will be weeping and grinding of teeth.' And to the centurion Jesus said, 'Go back, then; you have believed, so let this be done for you.' And the servant was cured at that moment.
(Matthew 8: 5-13)

REFLECTION

When you read this gospel story, I wonder how you feel about the encounter between Jesus and the Roman soldier. You may feel perplexed by Jesus' words, confused about what the soldier is saying, maybe you are comforted, challenged, jealous even that Jesus healed this man but hasn't healed somebody you want to be healed.

I believe that it is a beautiful case study in authority, power and the sensitive use of leadership.

It may be worth bearing in mind that in this encounter both
Jesus and the soldier were outcasts. Why do I say this? Well,
Jesus, for all his status as Rabbi and healer, was not accepted
by the Jewish authorities. Many of the scribes and Pharisees
showed open hostility to his ministry of inclusion and healing,
especially if it took place on the Sabbath. There were times in
the life of Christ where his very life was in danger, even before
he was eventually put to death. The powers that be were forever
trying to catch him out, exhausting every avenue of opportunity
to discredit and dishonour him.

The Roman soldier was also an outcast. Here we have a man, a
long way from home, a centurion serving his time with the
occupying army in Palestine. I cannot imagine for one moment
that he or any of his associates would have felt welcome in this
region. Their very presence on the streets of Capernaum would,
I'm sure, have aroused hostility, suspicion and animosity among
the locals. In his status as a gentile, he would not have been
allowed in the synagogues, nor do I believe he would have been
welcome in the markets or in the homes of any of the residents.
As a linguist I lived abroad for a year during my studies and
despite making friends, I often felt waves of homesickness, of
longing for a family meal, familiar British food and the
opportunity to speak my mother tongue with close relatives.

What a lonely place for this man to be! I wonder if he ever got
homesick or weary. So many details are left out in these gospel
accounts; nevertheless, I believe that the absence of these
particulars is there so that we will dive into our imaginations

and experiences to see what relevance his story has for us today.

What I love about this meeting between Our Lord and the soldier is that neither is afraid of nor intimidated by the other. The centurion could well have pressured Jesus into healing his servant, using his authority to coerce or even threaten the Lord. Conversely, Jesus could have shunned this man because of who he was and what he represented. He could easily have sent him on his way with a flea in his ear. But Jesus rejects nobody, not you, not me, not those we love or those who hurt us. Jesus' love is all-inclusive, no matter who you are or where you come from. That's the radical nature of the gospel. Jesus' mercy and compassion are universal; everybody is welcome in the Kingdom of God.

What I also love about this encounter is what the centurion says. He begins with a mark of supreme respect, using the word 'Sir'. So simple! A straightforward and deferential recognition of the authority and stature of Christ.

'My servant is lying at home, paralysed and in great pain.'

There are so many things that can keep us 'lying at home', locked within ourselves, paralysed and in pain. In my counselling work, I have come across many children whose anxiety is so great that they have been unable to leave their bedrooms for months on end or to eat with family and friends let alone attend school. This servant represents many in our world who live in physical or emotional agony, those who suffer paralysis of any kind, from birth or sickness, from accidents, abuse or mistreatment, from trauma or neglect. Maybe there is something which paralyses you, which needs the power of God's Holy Word to heal and transform.

See again how the centurion acknowledges the authority of Christ's healing ministry. He understands power and faith. Note too that, amazingly, this leader was seeking out Jesus for his servant. He doesn't tell Jesus what to do or how to do it. He simply names the problem. So often we use lengthy prayers, falling into the trap of telling God how to be God.

In 2019 a film was released starring Tom Hanks; its title is 'A Beautiful Day in the Neighbourhood'. The film centres on the American TV icon Fred Rogers. It's a lovely story about anger and forgiveness and in one scene Fred is swimming laps of his pool. As he does so he is praying in the simplest way possible. All he does is to name those whom he wishes to bring before God, one after the other.

Fred makes no requests and places no time restrictions on God's intervention; he asks for nothing. He simply names these people, trusting implicitly that God will know exactly what to do and when.

'My servant is lying at home, paralysed and in great pain.'

I love the way Jesus responds. He does not question the credentials of this soldier, he asks nothing in return for the favour; there's no bargaining or need for further explanation.

He simply offers to go and heal the man.

'I will come myself and cure him.'

What we have to remember here is that if Jesus had gone to the home of this soldier, he would have made himself ritually unclean and would have had to go through a purification ceremony in order to return to the temple. By offering to cure this unknown man, Christ was putting aside any personal inconvenience; healing and wholeness were at the heart of his ministry. His compassion never ceases to amaze me.

Once again we see the respect shown to Jesus by this soldier, 'Sir,' he says, 'I am not worthy to have you under my roof.' We use these words now during our mass, but what I particularly love about them is that here the centurion recognises who he is and who God is. This gentile, this man of war, whose authority had been procured by brutal means hardly possesses the perfect résumé for discipleship. And yet in this remarkable exchange, he shows us exactly what it means to follow Christ, to trust in his goodness and to leave the outcome to him.

'Just give the word and my servant will be cured.'

Jesus' word was enough. It will always be enough. When God's word is spoken, healing occurs. This man showed great faith because he believed that the word of Jesus was sufficient for his servant to be well.

To explain his understanding of this principle, the soldier then goes on to describe his own experience of authority and how the spoken word is enough for change to happen. This is a remarkable conversation and one that we would do well to heed. So often, authority is used to control, coerce, bully or force others to do our will. And yet here, it's seen as something restorative, life-giving and life-changing. Jesus only ever used his divinity to challenge those in power, to raise up the poor, to bring dignity and inclusion to those brought low, to heal and transform. At some deep visceral level, the Roman soldier knew this; no wonder Jesus was astonished!

I love too how Jesus publicly acknowledges the incredible faith of this foreigner, this pagan soldier. His belief is a miracle of God's grace. He is a living embodiment of what Jesus had come to bring about. 'Many', says Jesus, 'will come from the East and West to take their places with Abraham and Isaac and Jacob at the feast in the Kingdom of heaven.' In other words, God's Kingdom is not restricted to the people of Israel. God's Kingdom is for everybody, no matter who you are or where you live. Those who seek the will of God will always be recognised, accepted and welcomed.

Jesus also includes a warning here too, 'the subjects of the Kingdom will be turned out into the dark, where there will be weeping and grinding of teeth.' Maybe this was an attack on the Jewish authorities who failed to recognise who Jesus was. I think too though, that it is a caveat for us. If we remain stuck in the religiosity of faith, if we fail to welcome others in the name of Christianity, if we remain trapped in dogma and doctrine, then we can never fully know the liberating power of Christ for everyone, even for those we don't like or of whom we don't approve.

God looks not on the outward appearance, but only ever on the heart. As we see in this beautiful encounter Jesus is unimpressed by status. It makes no difference to him how others see us. God's love frees, heals and transforms.

'You have believed, so let this be done for you.'

FOR REFLECTION
- Are you in a position of authority? If so, how do you use it?
- Are you paralysed by something in your life? Do you need to ask for Christ's transforming love?
- Are you able to recognise the supreme authority of Christ?
- How do you pray? Can you simplify your prayer?

WE PRAY
- for all those in great pain
- for a deeper understanding of who we are and who God is
- for liberation from all that binds us.

Gentle Jesus,
May I always know that your Holy Word is enough to bring healing and wholeness. Help me to trust in your goodness, today and always. Amen.

PART THREE

ENCOUNTERING CHRIST

9. *MY EYES HAVE SEEN*

When the day came for them to be purified as laid down by the Law of Moses, Mary and Joseph took Jesus up to Jerusalem to present him to the Lord – observing what stands written in the Law of the Lord: every first-born male must be consecrated to the Lord – and also to offer in sacrifice, in accordance with what is said in the Law of the Lord, a pair of turtledoves or two young pigeons.

Now in Jerusalem there was a man named Simeon. He was an upright and devout man; he looked forward to Israel's comforting and the Holy Spirit rested on him. It had been revealed to him by the Holy Spirit that he would not see death until he had set eyes on the Christ of the Lord. Prompted by the Spirit he came to the Temple; and when the parents brought in the child Jesus to do for him what the Law required, he took him into his arms and blessed God; and he said:

'Now Master, you can let your servant go in peace, just as you promised; because my eyes have seen the salvation which you have prepared for all the nations to see, a light to enlighten the pagans and the glory of your people Israel.'

As the child's father and mother stood there wondering at the things that were being said about him, Simeon blessed them and said to Mary his mother, 'You see this child; he is destined for the fall and for the rising of many in Israel, destined to be a sign that is rejected – and a sword will pierce your own soul too – so that the secret thoughts of many may be laid bare.'

(Luke 2: 22-35)

REFLECTION
After all the excitement and movement that characterises
the beginning of Luke's gospel, we find this little family in
the temple of Jerusalem presenting their newborn to God in
accordance with the ancient Law of Moses. It reminds me of
Hannah presenting Samuel to the Lord and shows us once again
how Jesus is truly the fulfilment of the Old Testament (1Samuel
1:24-28).

With every gospel passage there are always two questions to ask
ourselves:

1. What is this telling us about God?
2. What is this telling us about discipleship?

Mary and Joseph are obedient to this ancient Jewish Law of
Purification and Presentation. According to Leviticus, a woman
is classed as unclean after giving birth and so Mary comes to
the temple for cleansing. She and Joseph bring with them the
offering of the poor. Traditionally it should have been a lamb
and a dove but the fact that they brought two doves suggests
that despite his lineage Joseph was not a rich man.

See how God meets us in our poverty; whatever we give to God
is taken, blessed and multiplied when our gifts to him are given
in sincerity and humility. God turns nobody away, no matter
who you are. Mary was holding in her arms God's only Son.
And yet in this beautiful and touching scene, she and Joseph are
not claiming any special privileges, but offering themselves and
the child to their Creator in simplicity and trust. We can learn a

lot from this modest introduction. When we humbly follow the Law of God, great things can and do happen.

Into this scene comes an old man, a man described as upright and devout. He was clearly familiar with the scriptures and lived his life accordingly. However, there was something extra that marked him out from the rest.

Simeon had been looking forward to Israel's comforting; in other words, here was a man of optimism, faith and hope that God would fulfil his promises. How expectant are we in prayer? When God doesn't seem to act swiftly or to listen, how confident are we that he will respond and that we too will receive his comfort? Luke tells us that the Spirit of God rested upon Simeon. That same Spirit hovers over each of us too, by virtue of our confirmation. Do we ever stop to consider what this means? How aware are we of the gentle and comforting presence of God's Holy Spirit?

Simeon had all the qualities needed for discipleship. This elderly man had clearly spent much of his daily life in prayer and I can't help wondering how much of that prayer was spent in silence, listening and responding to the gentle voice of God. How else can you trust him? How else can you know when God speaks? How else can you know when and how to respond? I know that many times I have drowned out the voice of God in my prayer time; instead of using the words from Samuel (1 Samuel 3:10), 'speak Lord, your servant is listening', I have made them into 'listen Lord, your servant is speaking.'

For Simeon to have responded to the prompting of the Spirit on that particular day suggests to me a deep and intimate relationship with his Master, one of profound trust and openness to the outrageous and shocking possibilities that God presents to each of us. This is absolutely critical. Simeon listened and responded – a perfect duet for discipleship. What I also think is really beautiful is that Simeon did not write himself off; he didn't say, 'Oh I'm too old' or 'No, I won't go; I'm so tired right now'. Nor did he say, 'I've prayed already this morning, that will do for today.' No, he kept the Holy Spirit with him at all times, not switching on and off when it suited. Fidelity and trust were the hallmark of this man's incredible faith. We can learn so much from the wisdom of our elders.

I love to imagine this old man making his way into the temple, vigilant and ready for action, like a true disciple. Remember too, that the temple is the place where God dwells. And so this is symbolic in that Simeon is bringing himself into the presence of the Almighty, both figuratively and literally. In my mind I can see Simeon looking around and asking God to point out who and where the Christ would be. Was the temple busy that day or was it quiet? I wonder if Simeon had ever imagined the Messiah to be a weak and vulnerable baby in the arms of a poor teenage mother and her new husband. What would you have thought in his place? Can we see from this that God is in everyone, from the greatest to the least? Do we recognise him in our brothers and sisters?

This story tells us all we need to know about discipleship and about God. God does the most extraordinary things in the most ordinary circumstances. Anybody else in the temple that day would never have known who Jesus was if Simeon had not responded to that prompting of the Spirit. It is in the simple living of our daily, mundane lives that God breaks through, offering hope, salvation and comfort. It matters not what we do but how we do it; everything can be done to the glory of God.

We all need God's Holy Spirit in our lives, right here and right now. Otherwise how can others know who Jesus is unless we, like Simeon, proclaim him as the Messiah? How awesome would it be if others could look at us and know that the Holy Spirit was resting on us, the way it did on Simeon? Can we make a resolution here and now to ask for this grace? Can we radiate the joy of this Spirit in our lives?

I love too the image of Simeon taking the child into his arms. This old man at the end of his life recognises in this newborn infant the one who was to come into the world. And notice Simeon's beautiful prayer, the one we now call the Nunc Dimittis, meaning 'Now you dismiss.'

'Now Master you can let your servant go in peace.'

Simeon is not asking for a longer life so that he can monitor what happens to this child. He's not asking for the opportunity to keep in touch with the family. In this astonishing and humble prayer Simeon recognises the wisdom of the Almighty and is able to let go completely, to surrender his life and death to the one who has stayed by his side and fulfilled his promise. Simeon is able to fall into the arms of God's grace as he holds the child in his own arms. Simeon knows that his work is done and that God is in control. There's no fear of death, just a simple resignation to the will of God. I find this truly awe-inspiring.

What also amazes me about this prayer is Simeon's recognition that God has kept his promise as indeed he keeps every promise. He takes no glory for himself but returns it all to God for his fidelity and loyalty. Who knows how many times Simeon may have doubted God and wondered why it was taking so long? God's timing is perfect.

I love that Simeon gives this family the gift of his blessing. What a beautiful, stunning and yet simple reflection of God's love for us to emulate. Not only that, but he gives thanks to God that this gift is not just for himself but for all the nations, for pagans and Jews alike. God makes no distinctions but showers his great mercy on all of us, no matter who we are, what faith we follow, where we live or what we have done; his love is without borders, infinite and everlasting. We only need to look at the cross to see this.

In his gift of prophecy, Simeon recognises what the future holds for Jesus and for Mary. Jesus will bring division because of the radical nature of his gospel. Mary's soul will be pierced because she was the first disciple and because discipleship demands a laying bare of the soul, of facing up to who we are and of following a path which is counter-cultural and subversive. It's not easy but remember that we always have the comforting of the Holy Spirit to guide us and that God is always faithful to his promises.

FOR REFLECTION
- Can we see God bring extraordinary things out of the ordinary?
- Where and how do we meet God?
- How do we recognise the presence and promptings of the Holy Spirit?
- How willing are we to bare our souls before Jesus?

WE PRAY
- for the elderly, that their distilled wisdom may be treated with dignity and respect
- for newborn babies and their families, that they may be cherished and seen as precious gifts from our loving God
- for those who live a quiet and contemplative life, that the joy and comfort of the Holy Spirit will shine through them as they minister to our thirsty world.

Lord,
Thank you for the gift of Simeon and for his example of discipleship and trust in your goodness. Help us to emulate him and to surrender our lives and our deaths to you in simplicity and truth.
Amen.

10. *EPHPHATHA – BE OPENED*

Returning from the district of Tyre, Jesus went by way of Sidon towards the Sea of Galilee, right through the Decapolis region. And they brought him a deaf man who had an impediment in his speech; and they asked him to lay his hand on him. He took him aside in private, away from the crowd, put his fingers into the man's ears and touched his tongue with spittle. Then looking up to heaven he sighed; and he said to him, 'Ephphatha', that is, 'Be opened'. And his ears were opened, and the ligament of his tongue was loosened and he spoke clearly. And Jesus ordered him to tell no one about it, but the more he insisted, the more widely they published it. Their admiration was unbounded. 'He has done all things well,' they said, 'he makes the deaf hear and the dumb speak'.
(Mark 7:31-37)

REFLECTION

If you look at a map of Palestine during Jesus' ministry, you will see that to get from Tyre to the Decapolis region you would simply head south east. Sidon, however, is north of Tyre and the Decapolis region and is non-Jewish territory. Mark does not make it clear where this healing took place but he shows Jesus making a considerable detour in order to heal this man. The more I read of the gospels, the more I see that Jesus always has his own agenda, that he frequently bucks the trend of social norms, that his timing is perfect and that he knows exactly what he is about.

If I were going from Tyre to the Sea of Galilee, I'd want the most direct route. But Jesus has an appointment with the deaf and dumb man; I like to think of it as an appointment pencilled into God's diary at the beginning of time. With Jesus, there is no such thing as a 'chance encounter', no such thing as 'coincidence' or 'fate'. It's planned with love and compassion before the world ever began and delegated to his precious Son, Jesus, the wounded healer.

Who brought this man to Christ? Who are the anonymous 'they'? We don't know. It could have been his family, his friends, his neighbours or members of his community. Which one of them asked Jesus to lay his hand on him? Often these details are left out of the gospel accounts and I believe that this is quite deliberate since it gives us the opportunity to question, ponder and imagine these events for ourselves. It can often be so helpful to place ourselves in the story too.

Did the man come willingly? I know some people who are ill but who feel they don't want to get well, because if they did, they fear that nobody would call in – or that they would have to work when they have lost confidence in their ability to hold down a job. Sometimes, people who are disabled see it as a part of themselves; their identity becomes tied up with the infirmity in a good or a bad way and there is nothing necessarily wrong with that. It's also possible that this man had visited other physicians without success and had lost hope in recovery. All these encounters tell us as much about ourselves as they do about the person of Christ.

There are many times in my own life that I feel terribly afraid to bring somebody to the Lord. I think that I am going to be ridiculed or rejected if I suggest to another that they might come to church. I fear humiliation if I offer to pray for them. And yet I am more than happy for others to pray for me. I even ask them to do so!

In this day and age we doubt the possibility of a miracle. It's easy to place more hope in medical staff than in the Lord. We forget that we are all made by God and that there is nothing he cannot put right. Not one thing. His healing, transforming power didn't stop at the crucifixion. Do we believe this? Can we approach that throne of sublime grace willingly and with confidence?

Not only that but I wonder how aware we are that Jesus' healing is not simply about curing infirmities. Rather, it's about helping us to understand just how loved we are by God. Sometimes the outcome of prayer is less about a change of situation and more about a transformation of the heart.

Let me go back to the story. We know that people with a hearing impediment often feel cut off from society. It's difficult to follow a conversation when you can't hear it, particularly if there is any background noise. We sometimes criticise the hard of hearing for having the TV turned up too loud or for pretending they have heard the question we asked and for giving a wrong answer. Those with other difficulties can also find themselves the butt of people's jokes. I had a speech impediment until I was

12 and I can remember being teased mercilessly for it. I still am from time to time.

I know that I am guilty of excluding others from my social interactions when they don't fit into the norm. I have stood by and watched a person being ridiculed for something that was not their fault. I think we are probably all guilty of this.

We read that Jesus took this man to one side. Why? I believe there are two reasons:

1. Jesus recognised how hard it would have been for this man to be in a crowd when he was used to social isolation. This shows empathy at a very deep level.

2. I also believe that Jesus wanted to emphasise to this man how special he was to God. That is a huge message especially when you are on the margins of society.

There is something here for me too about the power of silent prayer. I once heard it said that words are a curse to prayer. Imagine this man, looking at the beautiful face of Jesus, unable to hear his words and unable to communicate any words of his own. What does that matter to Our Blessed Lord? The man had no need to tell Jesus anything because Jesus already knew.

Maybe there is a message here for each of us, to make time to be alone and in silence with our Creator. How else can we possibly know how special we are to him – we who are made in the image and likeness of God himself? Can we come before God, knowing that he will take care of all our needs in the way he wants to?

Jesus heals this man with his touch. In those days anyone with a disability was seen as a sinner, shunned by the community and left on the margins of society. The belief held amongst the Jews of these times would have been that the man, his parents or ancestors had sinned. And so I imagine that he, isolated from his peers by his impediment, would have longed for the touch and acceptance of another. And Jesus knew this. The way Jesus heals this man is incredibly intimate, almost shocking.

It reminds me of when my son was a small baby and he used to sit on my knee looking at me, his hands all over my face, in my hair, my ears and my mouth. In those days before he could speak, I believe this was his way of telling me how much he loved me and wanted to be a part of me.

Not many of us would allow a stranger to touch us in this way. But what really blows me away is that the man did permit Jesus not only to put his fingers into his ears but to touch his tongue with his own spittle. Even Jesus' spittle has the power to heal and transform! How awe-inspiring is that? I wonder, though, why Jesus chose to use this method. Two reasons come to my mind:

1.   With God nothing is wasted, not even spittle.

2.   By putting his fingers into the man's ears and by touching his tongue in this way, Jesus is sharing his

words with this man in a deeply symbolic and intimate
manner. The first words the man heard would have
been the words of Jesus; the first words he would have
spoken would have been the words of Christ. And so,
Jesus is empowering this man to be his disciple. Isn't
that quite sublime?

God can use every part of us; with him nothing is wasted. And
I think that what this story is teaching us is that Jesus longs for
a deep spiritual intimacy with each of us. I believe that Christ
wants to touch and open our ears; that he wants to touch and
loosen our tongues so that we can hear and speak his words –
words of compassion, love, acceptance and peace. His healing
of this outsider shows that God's love is for everyone.

Jesus looked up to heaven, recognising that all authority had
been given to him by his Father and said, 'Ephphatha', 'Be
opened'. Wow! I love the minimalism of Christ. One word, one
touch and everything is changed. We complicate it, he keeps it
simple.

Jesus then orders them to tell nobody about it. Here is our
servant king, refusing to engage in religious power politics,
urging the crowd to silence in case false popular support was
aroused, never needing a majority, desiring only to do the will
of God and turning our world upside down. I love it!

Their admiration was unbounded. 'He has done all things well,'
they said, 'he makes the deaf hear and the dumb speak'.

FOR PERSONAL REFLECTION
- Do we recognise when it's time to speak and when it's time to listen?
- Is your admiration for Christ unbounded?
- Do you look to heaven for guidance when you need strength?
- Is there something you would like to say to Jesus here and now?
- Is there something Jesus wants to say to you here and now?

WE PRAY
- for those who bring others to God that they may continue to show courage and trust
- for the deaf and dumb and all those who work with them; that they will hear and know the gentle voice of God
- for those on the outskirts of our society, that we may extend to them the preferential and inclusive love of Christ.

Gentle Jesus,
Thank you for the gift of your touch. Thank you for showing us how precious we are in your sight. We ask you to touch our ears, that we may hear your words; we ask you to touch our tongues, that we may speak your words of love and compassion. And we ask you to touch our hearts, that we may be inspired to follow you, today and always. Amen.

11. THE DEVIL HAS GONE OUT OF YOUR DAUGHTER

Jesus left Gennesaret and set out for the territory of Tyre. There he went into a house and did not want anyone to know he was there, but he could not pass unrecognised. A woman whose little daughter had an unclean spirit heard about him straightaway and came and fell at his feet. Now the woman was a pagan by birth and Syrophonecian, and she begged him to cast the devil out of her daughter. And he said to her, 'The children should be fed first, because it is not fair to take the children's food and throw it to the house-dogs.' But she spoke up: 'Ah yes, sir,' she replied, 'but the house-dogs under the table can eat the children's scraps.' And he said to her, 'For saying this, you may go home happy: the devil has gone out of your daughter.' So she went off to her home and found the child lying on the bed and the devil gone.
(Mark 7: 24-30).

REFLECTION

Today's gospel may not sit well with our image of Jesus as the gentle, approachable Son of God. At first glance you may, as I did, find Jesus' response to this woman harsh and a little rude.

But, as is the case with so many of the gospel stories, there is always more. And the more we sit and ponder, the more we learn.

At the beginning of the story we find Jesus in the region of Tyre. Why Mark puts him there is unclear but we are told he didn't want anyone to know where he was. Why was that?

When Jesus was born in the stable at Bethlehem he became man. It's easy to think of Jesus as the second person of the Trinity, the Son of God: but remember that he was fully divine and fully human. He took on our humanity in all of its facets.

So maybe Jesus didn't want anyone to know where he was because he wanted a day off. He needed to rest and pray, to recuperate in solitude and peace. Does that ring a bell with you?

Maybe Jesus was exhausted and stressed, maybe his feet were sore with all the walking around; perhaps he was travel weary or a little bit homesick. Maybe the disciples were getting on his nerves or he was fed up of arguing with the scribes and Pharisees! It could be that he wasn't well – he could have eaten something that didn't agree with him, or, dare I say it, drunk a bit too much wine. Or maybe he was coming down with flu! Who knows?

I think that what Mark is telling us here is that there is nothing we could ever feel that Jesus doesn't know about. So often, we find ourselves rushing around, doing things for God or for others. Service has its place, of course it does. But do we run the risk of keeping so busy that we forget to hear God's still, small voice that beckons us to peace and solitude? God needs to take his place in our lives too; he longs to speak to us in the silence of our hearts. And so maybe Jesus going to this region of Tyre was because he needed to be alone with his Father, without the crowds. Not only that, but Jesus' ministry was about example. And so by doing this, he was showing his disciples that they too will need to take a break at times and to listen to what God is saying. It's all about balance. Could this passage be saying something to you?

Enter the woman. In some translations, the woman is described as gentile; here she is described as pagan. A gentile is simply a non-Jewish person whereas a pagan belongs to no major recognised religion. To me this bears significance as it shows the lengths to which Jesus will go in order to include everyone. Nobody is outside the mercy and healing of God, no matter who you are, where you live, what your gender or social status is or what you profess to believe. God is love and Jesus is the manifestation of that incarnate love which is for all people.

What also interests me is that Mark doesn't tell us the name of this woman. Have you ever noticed that so many of the gospel characters are left anonymous? Why is that? I believe that what Mark is trying to tell us is that the message is more important than the name. It gives universality to his stories, showing us that Jesus came for everybody. His gospel stretches across time and space, including everyone and excluding no-one.

This mother is one audacious woman whose desperation had become her strength and courage. A woman who dared to bypass all social etiquette in her quest for healing for her daughter. In those days being a woman would have signalled social inferiority, political inequality and exclusion from any religious decision-making. You couldn't get much lower than a pagan woman. To approach Jesus like this would have been a scandal. However, it is only when we touch the scandal of Christ's ministry that we can truly touch its beauty and power.

And yet, I think that this woman knew. I think she knew that she wasn't just approaching a Jewish rabbi, but that somehow she was approaching the throne of grace.

Look at what she does. She doesn't stand before the Lord, she doesn't look him in the eye; she assumes no equality with him, she simply falls at his feet in humility and desperation, recognising his divinity and her poverty. She's not pretending to be anything she isn't; she's coming just as she is, in exactly the way Jesus wants us to approach him – just as we are.

So often we fall into the trap of thinking we have to 'get ourselves right' before we can come to prayer. It's not what God wants. He wants only to meet us wherever we are, spiritually, emotionally, physically. Such a beautiful thing!

The little daughter has an unclean spirit in her. Imagine that in one so young. To suffer in that way from such an early age is very sad. What does it mean to have an unclean spirit within? How has this manifested itself in that child? What behaviour has that woman had to endure day after day? Verbal abuse? Physical abuse? Insults, spitting, tantrums? Has the daughter run away? Set fire to things? Damaged the home? Thrown stones? In my counselling work with teenagers and their families I have seen and heard many examples of challenging and difficult behaviour at home, of young girls and boys screaming and swearing at their parents, of furniture being broken, homes trashed, relationships damaged, injuries inflicted by the children on their care-givers. On-screen violence can so often be at the heart of this conflict.

And what of the family of this pagan woman? I can only imagine the isolation they must have felt in the community. Ostracised, criticised. When we see poor behaviour in children it's easy to blame the parents. I don't imagine for one minute that this woman's daughter was ever invited to anyone's house for lemonade and birthday cake, let alone a pyjama party.

She's desperate. When we too are desperate, we need to know that Jesus is there to help us in our need. This account, whilst seeming to be a rather harsh conversation between Our Lord and the pagan woman is actually a lesson in perseverance, in what it means to keep the channels of communication with God open, no matter what the outcome.

In response to her request, Jesus tells her that it's not fair to take the children's food and throw it to the house-dogs. How rude! However, what we have to remember is that in those days, dogs were not seen as part of the family as they are now. Dogs lived outside the family home and so the comparison was not meant to dehumanise this woman but rather to emphasise the place of the Jewish people in God's saving plan. Jesus' primary mission was to Israel.

The problem with reading a text like this is that we cannot know what Jesus' facial expression was like when he was conversing with this woman. I like to picture him with a smile curling the corners of his mouth, a twinkle in his eye and a sense of irony and humour in his voice.

Maybe she saw this too, because look at her response. She is so bold! And so determined! She's not gone away thinking 'well you didn't answer my prayer so that's it – I'll never ask again.' How much can we learn from her about the power of persistent prayer?

I love her sharp-witted, clever response: 'But the dogs under the table can eat the children's scraps.' Instead of being offended she has the humility to rise above anger and indignation at what Jesus says. A wonderful example of bold and expectant prayer!

Think about this. She doesn't want the world; she's not asking to take her place at the table, she's not asking for the banquet; the crumbs are enough.

Here she is, a mother on her knees before God incarnate, wanting this one thing – not even for herself but for her precious, beloved daughter, asking for this child not to be under the power of the Evil One, but to live in peace and freedom under the power of Almighty God.

God loves you and he loves everyone, regardless of your race, colour, background, religion or social standing. Nobody is insignificant to God. This story illustrates my point. Christ turns nobody away.

If it's good enough for him, is it good enough for you?

FOR PERSONAL REFLECTION

- Can you approach God just as you are?
- How do you respond when your prayer is not answered in the way you'd like it to be?
- How persistent are you in prayer? Do you need to ask for the courage of this pagan woman?
- Are you aware that God wants only what is best for you?

WE PRAY

- for all those trapped in the power of evil. Lord, grant them your freedom
- for those on the margins of society, that they may know, through our example, the inclusive and inexhaustible love of God
- for parents, especially those whose children are sick in mind or body.

Loving God,
You turn nobody away; everyone is precious to you. Help me to understand that you hear all our prayers, even when it doesn't feel that way. Give me the grace to keep going and to trust you with all those I love, knowing that you only want what is best for your creation. Amen.

11. *IF I CAN TOUCH THE HEM OF HIS CLOAK*

When Jesus returned to the other side of the lake, a great crowd gathered around him. Then one of the leaders of the synagogue named Jairus came and, when he saw him, fell at his feet and begged him repeatedly, 'My little daughter is at the point of death. Come and lay your hands on her, so that she may be made well, and live.' So he went with him.

As Jesus went along, the people were crowding him from every side. Among them was a woman who had suffered from severe bleeding for twelve years; she had spent all she had on doctors, but no one had been able to cure her. In fact, she was getting worse. She came up in the crowd behind Jesus and touched the hem of his cloak, for she said, 'If I can just touch the hem of his cloak I will be made well.' And her bleeding stopped at once, and she felt in her body that she was healed of her disease.

Jesus asked, 'Who touched me?' And his disciples said to him, 'You see the crowd pressing in on you; how can you say who touched me?'

But Jesus said, 'Someone touched me, for I knew it when power went out of me.'

The woman saw that she had been found out, so she came trembling and threw herself at Jesus' feet. There, in front of everybody, she told him why she had touched him and how she had been healed at once.

Jesus said to her, 'My daughter, your faith has made you well. Go in peace.'

(Luke 8: 40-48)

REFLECTION

I would like to begin by asking you to think about what you were doing 12 years ago and what has happened between then and now. Have you lost a loved one, seen the birth of a baby, watched your children grow up, changed jobs or retired, got a qualification, found or re-discovered God?

Where have you been? Have you moved house, been unwell, taken up a new hobby?

In 12 years, we will have experienced the sun rising and setting 4,380 times, eaten around 13,000 meals, and have taken over 74 million breaths.

For 12 years this woman had been bleeding.

I would also like to invite you to think about how much physical contact you have had in the last 12 years. If that's too much, maybe think about the last 12 days, hours or minutes. Who has kissed or hugged you? Who has reached out to shake or hold your hand? Who has touched your arm or put their hand in the small of your back, maybe as a gesture of comfort or concern? Who has stroked your hair, wiped a tear from your face or tickled your feet? On a more practical level, have you had a healthcare professional examine you? Or maybe you've had a pedicure, a manicure or a massage.

In those times, in that country, this woman would have been classed as unclean and untouchable. She would have been socially and spiritually isolated, unable to be out in public or to visit the synagogue. Imagine being banned from church. What must that do to a person's self-esteem? Not only can she not touch anybody but I don't imagine she would have been able to discuss her condition with others.

Even in today's society, in these times of 'enlightenment', it's not really the done thing to talk about women's stuff. It's embarrassing, it's taboo.

How did it start? Perhaps she'd just given birth and the bleeding never stopped. Maybe she'd always had problems. Who knows? It doesn't look like any of the doctors she'd spent her money on did. I wonder how many of them were bona fide professionals. All her money gone and the poor woman was getting worse.

I'm going to come back to this woman later. But first, let's have a look at Jairus, the synagogue official whose daughter is sick. We read that he fell at Jesus' feet and begged him to come to his house to heal his daughter. The cynic in me can't help wondering if he was one of the synagogue officials who criticised Jesus for healing a man on the Sabbath. Was he one of those who had questioned Jesus' credentials? We don't know. Maybe I'm doing the man a disservice. But what we do know is that nobody likes to beg. What man wants to throw himself at the mercy of another man and beg for his daughter's life? It's a humiliating experience, especially for a VIP. However, this man is desperate and what parent wouldn't put themselves through all manner of degradation to see their child well? Jesus loves this man. Jesus knows his pain. Jesus is Son of God and the Son of Mary. I believe with all my heart that Jesus learnt about compassion for the needy at the feet of his mother.

I want you now to imagine the scene in your mind. Jairus has found Jesus and has got him to agree to come and lay his hands on his sick daughter to make her well. But as they move, the crowd is pressing in. How hard must it have been for them to make any progress? A pressing crowd moves slowly. We all know that. And Jairus must have been beside himself with anxiety and worry. No flashing blue lights for this man! His daughter was dying. There was no time to lose.

But Jairus' daughter is not the only daughter who is sick. This woman is too. And so along she comes, haemorrhaging for 12 years, the same length of time as Jairus' daughter has been alive. And she says to herself, 'If I can just touch the hem of his cloak, I will be well.'

This woman, this unclean, lonely, ostracised, sick, penniless woman comes to Jesus, her last and only hope. Just look at the way she does this. Unlike Jairus, who approaches Jesus from the front and falls at his feet, she sneaks up from behind. She daren't address him; she can't address him on any level. 'If I can just touch the hem of his cloak'. She's not asking for or expecting Jesus' kiss or his embrace. That would make him unclean too. She's not asking for his touch or even his look. She just wants to make contact with the hem of his cloak, the bit of him that's furthest away from his body, from his hands, his heart and his head. She wants only to touch the bit of him that trails in the dust and dirt, the bit of him that gets wet and muddy when he steps in a puddle without raising his garments. She only wants to touch the bit of him that's frayed and tatty. That's all.

And how is she going to get to the hem of his cloak? She approaches the sublime throne of grace quietly, unobtrusively, humbly; by getting on her hands and knees and crawling through the crowd of people, pressing in on all sides, to approach Jesus from behind. She places herself physically exactly where she is emotionally. Life has brought her to her knees.

There's something too about the proximity of Christ that's enough for her. She's not got Jesus boxed off. The hem of his garment is enough to heal her of her 12 year infirmity. That's the power within him. No need to exchange words, no need to ask, to beg, bargain or demand. The sublime power of silent prayer. 'If I can just touch the hem of his cloak I will be made well.'

When Jesus realises the power has gone out of him, he asks, 'Who touched me?' Why does Jesus do this? A healing is so much more than a cure. Jesus is not only interested in the physical. He came to set the downtrodden free. By bringing her forward in front of this slow-moving, pressing crowd, he redeems her. He affirms her and restores her dignity. How amazing that he deals with the suffering, poverty stricken woman before Jairus the VIP! He raises her up to new life. In one simple sentence he puts right all the rejection, embarrassment, humiliation, all the pain and sorrow she's suffered for 12 long years. 'My daughter, your faith has made you well; go in peace.' He doesn't say, 'I have made you well', rather 'your faith has made you well.' Can you imagine how that must have felt to her, to have that given back to her with such generosity and love? And not only that, he calls her his daughter. At the start of the story, Jairus tells Jesus that his daughter is sick. It's like Jesus here is saying to Jairus, 'My daughter is sick too. She matters to me just as much as your daughter matters to you.'

Jesus came for everyone, even ritually unclean women who can't participate in ordinary life, women who are excluded and viewed as receiving punishment.

Jesus came for Jairus too. The good news is for everyone, even those who perpetuate the system that has ostracised the woman all these years. God is love. God is non-judgemental love. God is love for all those who aren't male, God is love for all children who aren't yet fully developed and who don't think that God is for them. God is love for the ones society doesn't love much. God is love for the high and low, it matters not. Unending love, amazing grace! What a powerful and empowering message for us all.

FOR PERSONAL REFLECTION

- Are you or is someone you know sick? Do you need to touch the hem of Jesus' cloak?
- Have you ever been ignored, dismissed or avoided for something that was not your fault? How did that feel?
- Have you ever rejected somebody because of their disability or infirmity? If so, do you need to ask for forgiveness?
- How do you approach Jesus?
- Are you aware of the height and depth of God's love?

WE PRAY

- for those who are sick in mind or body
- for all whom society rejects
- for a greater compassion towards the outcasts in our midst.

Gentle Jesus,
With you nobody is rejected. Nobody is unclean or untouchable. You love each of us with a love beyond anything we could ever ask for or imagine. We thank you for that love. And we ask that you set us free from all that binds us, from all that stops us living the life that you want for us. We ask for your healing, your grace, your tenderness, your mercy and your compassion. And we ask this knowing that you will answer our prayer in your time, which is both perfect and supreme. Amen.

13. *TODAY SALVATION HAS COME TO THIS HOUSE*

Jesus entered Jericho and was going through the town when a
man whose name was Zacchaeus made his appearance; he was
one of the senior tax collectors and a wealthy man. He was
anxious to see what kind of man Jesus was, but he was too short
and could not see him for the crowd; so he ran ahead and climbed
a sycamore tree to catch a glimpse of Jesus who was to pass that
way. When Jesus reached the spot he looked up and spoke to him:
'Zacchaeus, come down. Hurry, because I must stay at your
house today.' And he hurried down and welcomed him joyfully.
They all complained when they saw what was happening. 'He
has gone to stay at a sinner's house' they said. But Zacchaeus
stood his ground and said to the Lord, 'Look, sir, I am going to
give half my property to the poor, and if I have cheated anybody,
I will pay him back four times the amount.' And Jesus said to
him, 'Today salvation has come to this house, because this man
too is a son of Abraham; for the Son of Man has come to seek out
and save what was lost.'
(Luke 19:1-20)

REFLECTION

In this beautiful encounter from Luke's gospel we are
introduced to a wealthy man who wasn't just any old tax
collector; Zacchaeus was a senior tax collector in a wealthy and
prosperous city. In those days, tax collectors were notorious for
swindling and defrauding the town's residents and for taking
more than was fair. Therefore Zacchaeus and his entire family

would have been disliked, mistrusted and shunned by many of the townsfolk. As senior tax collector, Zacchaeus would have encountered fear and hatred probably on a daily basis.

I have met many people who reach positions of rank and authority and whilst this can bring status and wealth, it can also be a lonely place if one isn't careful. Even among his colleagues, I don't see that Zacchaeus would have had many friends. Not only that, but being small in stature, I imagine that he would have been the butt of others' jokes and I have no doubt that Zacchaeus himself would have been fully aware of this.

We read that Zacchaeus was anxious to see what kind of a man Jesus was. The word 'anxious' to me denotes a sense of panic and restlessness. I wonder if this anxiety went deeper than simply catching a glimpse of the Messiah. Maybe Zacchaeus was profoundly dissatisfied with the way his life had turned out; for all his wealth he was unpopular, isolated and, I suspect, terribly lonely. Here was an opportunity for change, for transformation and for the new life that Jesus was offering. And I guess at some visceral level, this wealthy, friendless senior tax collector knew that here was an occasion not to be missed.

Notice that it doesn't say he wants to meet or befriend Jesus. Was Zacchaeus hedging his bets at this point? I wonder if he had heard of Jesus' reputation. If so, what did he know and why was it so important for him to see Christ? His curiosity had certainly been piqued. Maybe he'd heard of Jesus' preferential love for the poor, of his compassion, of his gentleness and mercy, of his willingness to include everyone, particularly those on the margins of society, which, for all his wealth, Zacchaeus was.

In order to get a glimpse of the Lord, Zacchaeus hurries on ahead and climbs a sycamore tree. A sycamore tree is massive. It can grow up to 70 feet tall. Zacchaeus meant business!

Historically the sycamore tree is seen as a symbol of strength, protection, eternity and divinity. In Israel it can also symbolise regeneration. If we apply these thoughts then it's easy to see the deeper meaning Luke has here. We, like Zacchaeus, all need the strength and protection of God whose love is eternal; we can tap into that love through the humanity and divinity of Jesus. Not only that, but Zacchaeus' encounter with Christ was the start of his own spiritual regeneration, a radical new way of living and being.

I love the way Luke tells this story. Whoever said that the bible is boring? This scene is so humorous! Just picture a short, wealthy, prestigious man, pushing through the crowd to get ahead, probably sweating and panting with the effort, running to climb a tree. What must the onlookers have thought? The absurdity of it is not lost! Could you imagine a senior politician doing something as outrageous as that? And yet...

Have you ever done anything foolish for Christ? Have you ever gone out of your way to meet him? We can meet God by so many means. Prayer is not just about coming to church or kneeling down somewhere. It's not just about reciting what we have learnt or listing our petitions before him. People use drama, dance, theatre, painting, nature, music, song and silence to draw themselves into deeper communion with the Lord. There are many ways in which we can climb a sycamore tree for Jesus. God is not just the Master of Creation; he is the Master of Creativity and will meet us exactly where we are in whatever way we choose to serve or praise him.

For me too there is something in this story about taking risks. Zacchaeus, already the butt of others' jokes, was prepared to risk his status and reputation in order to simply see Jesus. I think that takes courage. When we go looking for Christ, it's always worth it!

I love to imagine Jesus stopping at the foot of this tree and looking up at this short senior tax collector. When I do so, I see the Lord with a smile on his face, almost shaking his head in disbelief, eyes wide open and dancing, with his gaze fixed upon this man. 'Zacchaeus, come down. Hurry, because I must stay at your house today.' Take a moment to consider these words and how Jesus says them.

Again, I like to see the laughter on the face of Christ, as if he's saying, 'come down you daft thing!' Did Zacchaeus hesitate for Jesus to say hurry? And the fact that Jesus says, 'I must stay at your house today' suggests a sense of urgency, as though Jesus knew what was in the heart of this tax collector. Know too that this is the only recorded occasion in the gospels where Jesus invites himself to the home of another.

Of all the people in that scene, the Lord chooses this one man, this outcast. He could have taken his pick of virtuous men and women from the huge crowds following him. I'm certain that many of them would have loved the privilege of feeding Jesus. To me this speaks of a longing of God to restore to dignity those who feel lost. This moment is so deeply intimate and special. Jesus had eyes for nobody else but this little man who'd climbed a tall sycamore tree merely to catch a glimpse of him. Did Zacchaeus expect this? I doubt it! Again the symbolism of this is striking, because God always gives us more than we could ever hope for. His generosity is utterly boundless. God wants only to give us what is good. His desire is to stay in the homes of our hearts, not just today but for always. Do we know this?

What is also interesting is what Jesus doesn't say. At no point in the whole of this narrative does the Lord condemn Zacchaeus. Not once does Christ highlight his failures and wrongdoings. There is no accusation, no finger pointing, no harshness or humiliation. He simply invites himself round! It's so simple! And Zacchaeus' response? He welcomes him joyfully.

Not so joyful are those who condemn the actions of Christ, those who have yet to grasp the purpose of his mission. Here we see indignation, resentment and misunderstanding for going to the house of a sinner. There are times when we find ourselves envious of the gifts God has given to another, instead of rejoicing in the ones He has so generously given to us.

Jesus the Wonder Counsellor does not judge; instead he allows this man the space and freedom to look into his own heart, to see the mess he's made of his life, to acknowledge his sinfulness and to make amends to those he's hurt. And so at the end of this encounter we hear the generosity of Zacchaeus himself; he vows to give half his considerable property to the poor and to pay back four times the amount he cheated from others. Finally Zacchaeus has understood that all he really needs in his life is Christ, that wealth and property mean nothing to him, that Jesus is the answer to all his deepest longing. He has found the pearl of great price. What an incredible transformation!

Indeed salvation has come to the house of Zacchaeus.

I would like to end this reflection with a legend about Zacchaeus and it goes like this: Every morning Zacchaeus used to get up very early and go out. His wife wondered what he was doing and so one morning she decided to follow him. From a distance she saw her husband go to the well and fetch a full bucket of water. Zacchaeus took this bucket to a sycamore tree and placed it on the ground. Then he cleared all the fallen leaves and debris from around the tree and watered it with the water he had fetched from the well. When he had done that, Zacchaeus stood back, gazing at it in awe and wonder. His wife approached him and asked him what on earth he was doing. Zacchaeus replied, 'this is the place where Jesus found me and the place where I found Jesus.'

FOR PERSONAL REFLECTION

- How and where do you meet Jesus? Is God calling you to a greater sense of creativity when it comes to him?
- Can you make room for Christ in the home of your heart today?
- Is there anything you need to do to say you are sorry to somebody you have hurt? Can you ask God for the grace to do this?

WE PRAY

- for those who want to know Jesus at a deeper level
- for the courage to 'climb a tree' for Christ
- for those who feel they are on the fringes of society, that they will find acceptance by our example of inclusion.

Loving Jesus,
You called Zacchaeus into a deeper relationship with you by your forgiveness and healing. Help us to know that we can always turn to you, no matter what we have done. Give us the grace to surrender to your will in our lives, today and always.
Amen.

PART FOUR

JUDGEMENT

14. *THERE IS SOMETHING GREATER THAN JONAH*
The crowds got even bigger and Jesus addressed them, 'This is a wicked generation; it is asking for a sign. The only sign it will be given is the sign of Jonah. For just as Jonah became a sign for the Ninevites, so will the Son of Man be to this generation. On Judgement Day the Queen of the South will rise up with the men of this generation and condemn them, because she came from the ends of the earth to hear the Wisdom of Solomon; and there is something greater than Solomon here. On Judgement Day the men of Nineveh will stand up with this generation and condemn it, because when Jonah preached, they repented; and there is something greater than Jonah here.
(Luke 11:29-32)

REFLECTION

A number of years ago I was listening to a talk by Anne Graham Lotz, the daughter of the evangelist Billy Graham. In it she said this:

> When you read the scriptures remember...
> If there is a promise – claim it.
> If there is a command – obey it.
> If there is encouragement – accept it.
> If there is a warning – heed it.

I wonder what this reading is saying to you.

In the Old Testament Jonah is sent by God to the Ninevites with a plea for repentance (Jonah 3:1-10). God is angry with his people for their wickedness and disobedience to his law and is threatening disaster. At first, Jonah tries to run away from God and ends up in the belly of a whale for three whole days, before being spewed up onto the beach. From there, Jonah's eventual obedience is instrumental in averting that punishment, because as we know, God relents and does not inflict on them the disaster he had threatened. There is the command that Jonah has obeyed. If you ever get the chance, the book of Jonah is a good read. It's short and would probably take no more than ten minutes from start to finish. But the resounding message in this book is that God is merciful and forgiving. God is God of the second chance, and indeed the third and the fourth – right into infinity. That is the encouragement we are invited to accept.

God said to Jonah 'Up, go'. A short and succinct message that maybe he's saying to you and me today. If so, it's a command for us to obey. I know that sometimes we're afraid of witnessing to our faith. All too often we feel that we have to do this by our own strength, forgetting that God will give us whatever we need, whenever and however we need it. The call to spread the message of the gospel is offered to all of us by virtue of our baptism. I have heard people tell me that they are afraid of this call because it might mean having to go and live else-where, to leave everything behind. And maybe it will; but more often we are simply invited to grow where we are planted, to be a presence of hope, gentleness and peace in our everyday lives.

Please remember that the people of Nineveh believed God's message, not just because of Jonah, but because God had got there first. He had already opened the minds and hearts of the Ninevites to accept what Jonah had to say. God is master of time and space. There is nowhere that you and I could ever go to that he's not visited and there is no person that we could ever speak to that God has not already spoken to. Evangelisation is his work – you and I are his chosen instruments. All God asks for is an open heart and a willingness not to preach, but to share something of what it means to us personally to follow Jesus, by the way we speak and act.

After the Ninevites had repented, Jonah becomes angry with God for being so compassionate and loving towards them. And we're sometimes like that too. Maybe there is a warning here for us to heed. I've heard people say that we should bring back capital punishment, lock up offenders and throw away the key. I've heard people say that we should bring back corporal punishment in schools; that it's okay to hurt children to make them behave. It's not God's way. He never creates an appetite for violence. We do that. God takes no pleasure in the death of a wicked man but in the turning back of a wicked man who changes his ways to win life (Ezekiel 33:11). That's what the Ninevites did. They changed their ways to win life. That's God's method. That's God's forgiveness.

I believe that wrongdoings are not so much sins that need to be punished; rather they are wounds that need to be healed. I think too that this sums up the heart of our beautiful God who loves us all implicitly and unconditionally.

In this gospel passage, Jesus is angry at the crowds because they asked for a sign. If we rewind slightly, Luke tells us that Jesus has just cast out a demon and the crowd accuse him of having done that by the power of the devil (Luke 4:35). Unlike the people of Nineveh the crowd want a miracle from God to affirm Jesus' authority. What kind of miracle did they want? Was the exorcism not enough? I wonder how they saw Jesus. What was he to them?

You see, faith in miracles isn't really faith. What Luke wants us to understand is that what really matters is our relationship with a God who loves us. Not only that but he wants us to focus on the sign, that just as Jonah went into the belly of the whale, so will Jesus go into the tomb and that we are invited to share this paschal mystery.

Who is Christ to you? What do you want from him? I know that in my own life there have been many times when I have asked the Lord for a sign when I have felt lost or abandoned or when I have been trying to discern what God is saying.

One thing I will say is that there are signs of God's love all around us; we just need eyes to see them.

How do you see God? And how do you think he sees you? Perhaps there's a promise we can claim or encouragement we can accept. Or maybe there's a gentle warning for us to heed.

Jesus condemns the crowd because the Queen of the South

travelled a long distance to hear the Wisdom of Solomon. And there is something greater here.

It often seems to me that true wisdom is about knowing who God is and who we are. When the people of Nineveh sat down in sackcloth and ashes, I think that what they were doing was acknowledging how far removed from God they had become. As I said earlier, God loves us unconditionally. He is not an angry God who needs to be appeased by our sacrifices, our idols and our religious practices. God is a God who desires intimacy with each of us, a God who calls us by name and invites us to 'metanoia', to a change of heart, of mind and of will. When we stop asking for signs and simply see them all around us, in the love of one another, in the beauty of creation, in the kindness of a stranger, in new life, in the tiny minutiae of our daily lives, only then can we tap into the power and wisdom of our loving Creator.

Jesus is the Wisdom of God. He came to earth to show us how infinitely loved we are. Our Lord came in humility and poverty, born in a stable at Bethlehem and crucified on a hill outside Jerusalem. Christ went to the end of love not so much to atone for our sins but to show us just how much we are loved. There is no greater love than this, to lay down one's life for one's friends (John 15:13). Let me say this again: Jesus is the Wisdom of God.

How far are we willing to go to hear and gain that wisdom? How do we approach this sublime throne of grace? Do we come to Jesus with our shopping list of miracles we'd like him to perform for us or do we simply come as we are, ready to trust and to accept the graces he's already planned for us since the beginning of time? Are we ready to claim his promises and accept his encouragement, to heed his warning and obey his commands?

Jonah initially refused to do what God wanted. Jesus was obedient to death.

Jonah ran away from God. Jesus took every opportunity to spend time with the Father, drawing encouragement and strength from his fountain of love and mercy.

Jonah was frail and human. Jesus is powerful and divine.

Jonah put the lives of others in danger by his cowardice. Jesus sacrificed his life to set us free from sin and death.

Jonah was angry at the forgiveness and mercy of God. Jesus is the living embodiment of the forgiveness and mercy of God.

Jonah was in the belly of the whale for three days. Jesus was in the belly of the tomb for three days.

Jonah was spewed up on the beach. Jesus is risen in glory.

Jonah isn't here. Jesus is.

There is something greater than Jonah. Jesus is here.

FOR PERSONAL REFLECTION
- What is this passage saying to you about the power and authority of Christ?
- Are you looking for signs and wonders from Jesus?
- How much can you trust the wisdom of God?
- Do you really want the intimate relationship with God that Jesus offers? If so, what do you need to ask of him?

WE PRAY
- for missionaries in our own country and overseas. We ask you to renew them with your courage and wisdom that they may bring more souls to you
- for those who are trapped in sin. We ask that they may come to experience your deep well of forgiveness and mercy
- for those who do not know or acknowledge you, Lord. We ask you to open those hearts and minds to accept your promises and your words of encouragement
- for strength and resolve in our desire to draw ever closer to you
- that we may bear witness to God with courage and wisdom by what we say and what we do.

Loving and Creator God,
Thank you for the gift of your Son Jesus. Help us to follow him faithfully, to heed his warnings, obey his commands, accept his encouragement and claim his promises. We ask this in total trust of your loving mercy.
Amen.

15. *THE DEMAND WILL BE MADE FOR YOUR SOUL*

A man in the crowd said to Jesus, 'Master, tell my brother to give me a share of our inheritance.' 'My friend,' he replied, 'who appointed me your judge, or the arbitrator of your claims?' Then he said to them, 'Watch, and be on your guard against avarice of any kind, for a man's life is not made secure by what he owns, even when he has more than he needs.'

Then he told them a parable: 'There was a rich man who, having had a good harvest from his land, thought to himself 'What am I to do? I have not enough room to store my crops.' Then he said, 'This is what I will do: I will pull down my barns and build bigger ones, and store all my grain and my goods in them, and I will say to my soul: My soul, you have plenty of good things laid by for many years to come; take things easy, eat, drink, have a good time.' But God said to him, 'Fool! This very night the demand will be made for your soul; and this hoard of yours, whose will it be then?' So it is when a man stores up treasure for himself in place of making himself rich in the sight of God.'
(Luke 12:13-21)

REFLECTION

In the winter of 1989, my sister and I went on a week's package tour to Moscow. The highlight of our time there came towards the end of the week when our evening's entertainment was to visit the home of a Russian family. The selection procedure was a bit like speed dating. We all stood in the foyer of the hotel and waited to be approached by a native Muscovite. Fortunately for us, we were picked out by brother and sister team Boris and Natasha, who later told us that they had made a beeline for

Amanda and me because we 'looked fun'. Boris and Natasha took us on the trolleybus to a drab grey apartment block into a one bedroomed flat which they shared with their parents Aida and Viktor. Make no mistake about it, this was a poor family. However, the welcome, hospitality and kindness offered to us that evening was beyond anything we could have imagined.

Having lived and studied in the former Soviet Union, I know from firsthand experience the length of time that Aida would have spent queuing for the food she so generously laid out before us. I know too that Viktor would potentially have encountered problems sourcing the Russian vodka that poured so freely all evening. At the end of the night, Amanda and I were escorted back to our hotel wearing borrowed full-length fake fur coats on the promise that we would return them the following day. Aida was worried that our own coats were inadequate for the bitter cold.

I'm telling you this story because it is in direct contrast with the selfish and egocentric attitude of the Rich Fool in this parable of Jesus'. Where our Russian friends reached out to us in generosity, kindness, hospitality and welcome, sharing what little they had, this man concerns himself neither with God, nor with anybody else; he seeks only to satisfy his own desires.

At the beginning of this passage Luke gives us a somewhat strange comment made by an unnamed man in the crowd. He asks Jesus to mediate in some kind of financial dispute with his brother. Jesus responds with a very insightful question, 'who appointed me your judge?' When I first read this opening, I felt no small amount of irritation with this man. There are no social niceties, no inquiries after Jesus' health, no gratitude for his teaching, just this demand to sort out the disagreement he has with his brother.

However, on reflection I recognise in this parts of my own prayer life. I wonder if you do too. How often do we simply present our list of needs to the Lord, telling him what to do, how to do it and what the time frame for our request is? Are we more concerned with wanting God to change the hearts and minds of others to suit those of our own?

I believe that this man in the crowd has failed to understand who Jesus is and what his ministry is all about. Christ came to show us the face of God the Father. He was born into our world to reveal to us how loved we are – infinitely, wholly and eternally. Do we know this?

All too often I'm so focused on what I want God to do in my life that I forget to thank him for what he has already done. I don't always stop to praise and worship him simply for being God, a loving parent who always has my welfare at heart. I don't always pause to give God the space to speak to me personally and intimately. All we have is his gift. There is so much love and beauty in our world. We are surrounded by it every day if only we had eyes to see and ears to hear. I don't always take time to ponder that and to remember that this love is God's precious gift to each of us.

So perhaps there is a gentle challenge there. Could we spend some time in quiet prayer without asking for anything at all? Or perhaps if there is someone whose attitude we don't like, do we need to ask God to change in us what we would like changed in this other person? Do we need to ask for the grace to be less selfish, to be kinder, more patient or more forgiving?

Let me go back to this gospel passage.

I love the way Luke presents Jesus as a tender and loving teacher. Jesus never misses an opportunity to tell us about the Kingdom of Heaven. He is so clever! Look how he turns this man's demand into a lesson on values, showing us what really matters. He truly is the master life coach!

'A man's life is not made secure by what he owns.'

So why do so many of us think it is?

Of course it is true that we cannot take our possessions and wealth with us into eternity. But what I love most about this is how Jesus doesn't stop there but goes on to tell a story to illustrate his point.

This wealthy man has had a rich harvest from his land. He must have worked hard for this to happen, reaping and sowing, gathering his crops, buying and selling but always mindful of what needed doing and when. We need people like this; let's not forget that. If we want food on our tables, then an intelligent farmer is exactly what is required. Our food chains cannot survive without them.

However, it's the man's attitude to his success that Jesus warns us about. This rich man makes no mention of giving any of his surplus crops away to those who may need them more than he does. I believe that his heart is far from God. There is no spirit of generosity, inclusion, kindness or thought towards those less fortunate than he is. No – on realising how much grain he has amassed, he tears down the barns already there, probably perfectly serviceable and adequate for the job, then sets about replacing them with bigger ones to house this bumper crop.

This part of the story reminds me of the images we saw on our screens at the beginning of the Coronavirus pandemic. Long queues, supermarket shelves stripped bare of much needed goods, especially toilet roll. We witnessed the selfish hoarding of excess food while hospital staff, exhausted after long shifts were left scratching around for basic essentials. What an awful indictment on our society!

Again, is there another message for us in this story? Could we be less wasteful, more mindful of the way we treat one another and our planet?

The man then goes on to promise himself an easy retirement, full of food, drink and good times. Here Jesus doesn't say that the man isn't entitled to a rest after all his hard work. No, his message is very simple and it is this: we are not the centre of the universe. Life isn't simply about us, our wishes and our desires. With wealth comes responsibility. Everything we need is here. But if we ignore the cry of the poor, preferring instead to satiate our own excesses, then we are both spiritually impoverished and a long way from the Kingdom of God.

Not only that but this man addresses his soul directly, assuring it of an easy ride. Is not the soul God's dwelling place? If so, what need has God of rich food, drink and good times? God looks not on outward appearances but on the heart. The challenge is to listen to the still, small voice that dwells within, moving us to compassion and love.

At the end of the story the demand for this man's soul is made by God and the question asked, 'this hoard of yours, whose will it be then?' The simple answer is that it belongs to God. All we are and all we have are his. All is gift.

Jesus does not condemn the man for his wealth. He condemns him only for his attitude. When our focus is based on self, we cannot live in the freedom of God.

As I write this piece in 2021, we are coming out of the Coronavirus pandemic. Many have used this time to re-evaluate what matters most. We have seen heart-warming stories of compassion and generosity, of the old and young raising thousands for charity, of neighbours looking out for one another, of medical staff risking their own safety to care for their patients. We have witnessed communities coming together in a spirit of solidarity and unity, the rich and famous using their status to force social change, and families spending time together in the great outdoors. It is precisely in this attitude of heart that God's Kingdom is proclaimed.

FOR REFLECTION

- St Teresa of Calcutta once said:
  'I don't recall that the Lord ever spoke of success; he spoke only of faithfulness in loving.' Are we more concerned with wealth and status than with the Kingdom of God?
- Can we be more generous with what we have?

WE PRAY

- for those whose hearts are far from God
- for a deeper understanding and appreciation of the many gifts we receive from God every day of our lives.

Loving God,
You sent Jesus to show us how to live in your love. Help us to fix our gaze on you, present in our brothers and sisters. Give us the grace to share what we have with those in need so that we can become rich in your sight.
Amen.

16. *WHEAT AND DARNEL GROW SIDE BY SIDE*

Leaving the crowds, Jesus went to the house; and his disciples came to him and said, 'Explain the parable about the wheat and darnel in the field to us.' He said in reply, 'The sower of the good seed is the Son of Man. The field is the world; the good seed is the subjects of the kingdom; the darnel, the subjects of the evil one; the enemy who sowed them, the devil; the harvest is the end of the world; the reapers are the angels. Well then, just as the darnel is gathered up and burnt in the fire, so it will be at the end of time. The Son of Man will send his angels and they will gather out of his kingdom all things that provoke offences and all who do evil, and throw them into the blazing furnace where there will be weeping and grinding of teeth. Then the virtuous will shine like the sun in the kingdom of their Father. Listen, anyone who has ears!'
(Matthew 13:36-43)

REFLECTION

We may find ourselves asking why the disciples needed to ask Jesus to explain this parable to them when it's so blindingly obvious what he is talking about. So often we fall into the trap of thinking that we are all good; those who break the law are all bad. We assume that if we live a good life, we'll go to heaven; those who have done serious harm to others will go to hell. Please read on because it's not that straightforward.

There is often a danger that we can become very complacent about Jesus' parables, particularly when we have heard them a few times. The thing is, though, that with all Jesus' stories, there are layers of meaning which he gently invites us to explore. Whenever we take the time to do this, especially when we ask the Holy Spirit to guide and enlighten us, we are able to discover the hidden riches of Christ's teaching. There is always something new to learn, always the challenge to go deeper and to see as God sees.

The disciples remind me of those valiant children whom I have taught over the years who dare to ask for clarification when they don't understand. Admitting that you haven't grasped a point can be difficult, especially if you are self-conscious and afraid of ridicule. I have found that teenagers are especially susceptible to this. Nobody wants to be the one who admits to any lack of understanding. Thank God that the disciples did ask, because if they hadn't, we too could still be in the dark. There is no shame in asking Jesus for a deeper comprehension of his Holy Word. On the contrary, I think this is exactly what Christ wants.

In this parable Jesus tell us that the field is the world and he himself is the sower. Imagine Jesus with his bag of seed, liberally throwing it all over the place. He throws it on every piece of land and water, every mountain and every valley regardless of the season or climate. He throws his Word through time and space in an untiring bid to build up the Kingdom of his Father. The invitation to hear his Word is so generously given. The seed never runs out. Our faith is not exclusive; it's a free and bounteous gift for everyone.

What Jesus sows is good. We see that time and again; Jesus does nothing wrong. No evil is ever spoken by him and no action he takes can be interpreted as wicked or unkind. Jesus sows his good seed by his words, actions, invitations, by his prayer, his acceptance, his healing ministry and his forgiveness. What Jesus is sowing is love, a love so liberal and one that is offered with supreme munificence. We only need to look at the cross to see that.

Jesus longs to give this love to everyone – no exceptions, no conditions. His love is abundant, life giving and everlasting.

That bit's simple. But what about the good seed, the Children of the Kingdom? Who are they? How do we distinguish a Child of the Kingdom from a Child of the Evil One? You see, it's quite easy, isn't it, to assume that we are Children of the Kingdom. Maybe you come to mass or other church services, even on a weekday when there is no obligation. Perhaps you say your prayers, visit the sick, speak kindly to others, and put yourself out from time to time. There is nothing wrong with this; God loves that you love. Please know that. However, this ever persistent God is always calling us into deeper relationship. There is always the invitation to know him as the loving Father, to ALL people, not just the 'good ones'.

But what do we think about the Children of the Evil One? Are they the prisoners, the wrong-doers, the bombers and those who mug old ladies? Maybe it's just not that straightforward. Nothing ever is!

And so which camp are you in? Are you a Child of the Kingdom or can you be a Child of the Evil One? In other words, how much love do you show?

You see, I think I'm a loving, caring person but how much love do I show when

- my neighbour parks outside my house even though he has room on his own drive?
- a colleague keeps interrupting my very important work to tell me about her challenging son?
- someone who only comes to church once or twice a year has the audacity to sit in my bench?

The more I delve into the gospels, the more I see that judgement is not ours to dish out. That bit belongs to God. It's so easy to fall into the trap of thinking we know the heart of God when we don't. We are simply called to look at our own hearts and minds, to see where healing and transformation are needed. We need to ask ourselves which side are we on and on which side we want to be. I don't think many people want to be seen as Children of the Evil One. On the contrary there is more goodness in the world than wickedness; each of us would like to think that we're okay. But it's not that simplistic.

Change has to begin with me. Maybe we need to say this to our children when they rage against the injustices of the world. Change begins with me and can begin with me, only and if I stay close to Jesus and allow him to heal my wounds so that I can live as he wants me to live.

Satan is very good at mind games. He can so easily seduce us into thinking that what we do and say is perfectly reasonable, that somehow we are 'in the right'. And so there is always a call to re-examine our lives and behaviour. Was I kind? Did I show love in my encounters today? Do I think the best of people rather than assume the worst? Like 'Whack a Mole' this is an ongoing challenge. The good news however, is that we don't and can't do this in our own strength, but only in him who gives us strength (Philippians 4:13).

Let's just go back to the seed and consider it for a moment. A seed is so tiny, some you can hardly see. And think about where a seed grows. A seed goes into the ground, where it's sometimes cold, even frozen, it's dark, it's dirty and it's smelly. We don't know what a seed is doing whilst it's underground because we can't see it. And that's what the Word of Jesus does; it enters into the murkiness and chaos of our minds and hearts where it slowly, patiently and unobtrusively grows into something that brings forth beauty, nourishment, something we can see, smell and touch. As it grows, we have to prune the bits that prevent it from blossoming into the fullness of life. When we nurture the Word of God, take it to our hearts and live it, we can become Children of the Kingdom.

There's darnel in all of us; I'm certain of that. And the devil is subtle enough to plant it and convince us that it's not that bad. Wheat and darnel look very similar and it's difficult to distinguish between the two. But look what God does in this parable. He allows both to grow side by side. To me that speaks volumes about the patience of God who never stops reaching out in compassion and forgiveness, giving us chance after chance, grace upon grace.

The beauty of our Christian faith is that we can always trust in God's mercy. His forgiveness is unconditional and his clemency is everlasting.

At the end of time the wheat and the darnel will be separated and let's not forget that that task is reserved for God alone who sees into the hearts of all his people and who judges in perfect righteousness. We don't need to fall into the trap of taking that responsibility on ourselves. All we need to concern ourselves with are the wheat and chaff of our own lives and to ask God, in his kindness to enrich our wheat and destroy our darnel in the flames.

FOR PERSONAL REFLECTION
- How willing are you to ask the Holy Spirit for a deeper understanding of what the gospels mean?
- Where would you put yourself and others in this story? Is there something you can learn from that?
- Is there a particular grace you would like to ask Jesus to give you in light of what you have just read?

WE PRAY
- for a deeper understanding of God's precious Word, that it may penetrate our hearts and minds and bring us closer to the source of life

- for all those responsible for spreading God's Word and for building up his Kingdom here on earth. Give us courage and fortitude
- for all those who don't know God's loving mercy and forgiveness, that by our example we can be beacons of light in the darkness of despair and hopelessness.

Lord,
On the day of the harvest the straw is set aside; the chaff is blown away by the wind and the weeds are consigned to the flames. But the wheat, like sacks of gold, is gathered into the barn.

Lord, on the day of death, the harvest of my life will be poured out before you, wheat and chaff and weeds together. Let your wise hand sift through it and keep what is worth keeping. And with the breath of your kindness, blow the rest away.
Amen. (Anon)

17. OUR LAMPS ARE GOING OUT

Jesus said to his disciples: 'The kingdom of heaven will be like this: Ten bridesmaids took their lamps and went to meet the bridegroom. Five of them were foolish and five were sensible: the foolish ones did take their lamps, but they brought no oil, whereas the sensible ones took flasks of oil as well as their lamps. The bridegroom was late, and they all grew drowsy and fell asleep. But at midnight there was a cry, 'The bridegroom is here! Go out and meet him.' At this, all those bridesmaids woke up and trimmed their lamps, and the foolish ones said to the sensible ones, 'Give us some of your oil: our lamps are going out.' But they replied, 'There may not be enough for us and for you: you had better go to those who sell it and buy some for yourselves.' They had gone off to buy it when the bridegroom arrived. Those who were ready went in with him to the wedding hall and the door was closed. The other bridesmaids arrived later. 'Lord,' they said, 'open the door for us.' But he replied, 'I tell you solemnly, I do not know you.' So stay awake, because you do not know either the day or the hour.'
(Matthew 25:1-13)

REFLECTION

I have read that in Jewish custom a marriage was always arranged by the parents of both bride and groom, often whilst the couple were still children. The groom would get the home ready then come out to meet his bride. Nobody would know when the entourage would arrive and the fun was in trying to catch the guests napping. Unimaginable in this day and age!

Ten virgins would be chosen from the town or village to dance with him through the streets when the groom went to meet the bride. The dance would include the use of lamps which were basically sticks soaked in olive oil and set alight. The sticks would be dipped in the oil roughly every 15 minutes to keep them burning so that the dance could continue for prolonged periods of time.

I love the image of this. Marriages can and should be a reason for great joy - a joy to be shared by the community. Two people, so in love that they are ready to declare this love before God and before the assembly. The community ready to rejoice alongside them with music and dancing. I like too the idea of the groom preparing the home for his bride. All of this is deeply symbolic. In the Old Testament, marriage is often used as a symbol of God and his people.

In Isaiah we read this: 'as the bridegroom rejoices over the bride, so shall your God rejoice over you' (Isaiah 62:5).

In this parable ten young girls are chosen as bridesmaids and all ten take their lamps. All ten start the story on a level playing field. Sadly only half make it to the wedding feast. The parable ends with a warning and when Jesus gives a warning, we do well to heed it!

On first reading this gospel seems quite alarming with an element of meanness on the Lord's part when he excludes them at the end with the words, 'I do not know you.' So what is the significance behind it?

To me the ten bridesmaids represent all of us, male and female. The choosing of these ten symbolises our baptism. In baptism each of us receives our calling to follow Christ. We are, each of us, children of God and God is our Father.

Since many of us are baptised as infants, it may not be immediately obvious to us what the road ahead involves and what we may need to help us along that road. However, throughout the gospels Jesus constantly calls us to live in communion with him and with God. In every encounter Jesus shows us that we are children of God and that we are loved unconditionally by him. It's not always easy; Jesus never said it would be; however what he did do was promise to be with us until the end of time (Matthew 28:20). At Pentecost, God sent his Holy Spirit to guide and protect us. Like the bridesmaids, we are all called to serve and to follow the Lord.

The lamps each bridesmaid takes signify the other sacraments, Reconciliation, Eucharist, Confirmation, Marriage or Holy Orders and the Anointing of the Sick.

The symbolism continues with each element of this story: the lamps, the oil, and the two kinds of bridesmaids.

Through the sacrament of **Reconciliation**, we are called to repentance, a turning away from all that prevents us from living in the freedom of knowing that we are eternally loved by God. Rather than being a duty or a chore, reconciliation can be a sacrament of great joy in which we can truly celebrate the mercy and grace of our Heavenly Father.

Confirmation is seen as the opportunity to strengthen and deepen our faith with maturity and responsibility -- another reason for great joy and celebration.

Marriage and **Holy Orders** give us the chance to live out our calling as followers of Christ in a new way and the **Anointing of the Sick** can provide spiritual comfort in times of great vulnerability.

These sacraments, like the lamps, can be occasions for delight and rejoicing; many are celebrated in a very public way as an outward sign of our commitment to Christ and his church as well as giving us light in times of darkness and showing us the way, particularly when we're lost.

The oil is what we do with those sacraments, which are, in themselves, gifts from God, gifts so freely and abundantly given – no conditions, no price tag.

The bridesmaids who took the oil are the ones who not only avail themselves of God's gifts but use them to bring life, light, joy, laughter and dancing to others they meet on the way. These bridesmaids are the ones who recognise what a privilege it is to be chosen to build up God's Kingdom here on earth. But that involves some degree of responsibility – hence the flasks of oil.

The sensible bridesmaids are the ones who understand that a journey of faith does not always take place in the bright light of day; there will always be moments of darkness and discouragement for which a lamp is needed to help us see. Symbolically these are the ones who spend time with the Lord in prayer, reading his Holy Word, listening to what he has to say and living the life he wants us to live.

The five foolish bridesmaids preferred to travel light, without the extra oil. Why was that? Maybe they have no sense of responsibility, are incapable of forward planning or simply too carefree to be bothered with the burden of a flask of oil. Who knows? It's easy to assume that we are among the sensible ones, the ones ready for every eventuality. But I know that I often travel light, by-passing opportunities to share my faith with others, judging those who are not like me, putting my own desires first, failing to live up to my unique calling as a child of God and not understanding who he is and who I am in his sight.

Let's look at what these foolish ones do when the bridegroom fails to appear at the expected time. Here is an opportunity to go and get oil but they pass it by and, like the disciples in Gethsemane, fall asleep. Such a human response, but again how often do we fail to seize the opportunities given to us to bear witness to our faith? I know I do.

When the groom does turn up, these foolish girls declare, 'Our lamps are going out' rather than immediately owning up to having brought no oil in the first place. And to compound the error they then ask the sensible ones to share their oil – relying on external sources to bail them out of a difficult situation. How often do we ask for or desire the oil of another – wanting something our neighbour has instead of celebrating who we are in the sight of God?

When the groom goes into the wedding hall without the foolish bridesmaids, they are left demanding to be let in to a feast they have no right to attend. 'Open the door for us' is the cry. Where's the apology? Where is the acknowledgment of their failings? Where is their honesty, their humility, their sense of responsibility, their sadness at the missed opportunity of God's divine grace? Lost in a wave of laziness, arrogance and irresponsibility.

We cannot enter heaven on the salvation for which others have worked. We have to claim that for ourselves. As I said at the beginning, all ten start on a level playing field but only half make it and when Jesus gives a warning, we do well to heed it.

Jesus is the groom who comes to meet and greet his beloved ones and to accompany them into the wedding feast. We are all chosen and we are all given opportunities to take our place in glory.

So what is this piece saying? For me it's that we have to prepare spiritually. We cannot ride in on the coat tails of another. At the end of the day it is down to us individually because we will make that final journey alone. Through the grace of our baptism and by the gift of the sacraments we all have the tools. However, it's not enough to float about half heartedly, relying on others to do the work.

How badly do we want to attend the feast? Tough love, tough message!

Let's pray for the grace and courage to accept our part in that.

FOR PERSONAL REFLECTION
- Do you want to attend the feast?
- What graces do you need to ask for in order to get there?

WE PRAY
- for all the baptised, that they may live up to their calling as sons and daughters of God, working tirelessly to build his Kingdom
- for those who have lost faith in God. May our witness give them hope and confidence in his abiding and loving presence
- for those who are lost in the darkness of despair, particularly those in prison or who suffer from mental illness or addiction
- for those who have died, especially those who have nobody to pray for them, that they may all share God's glory.

O my God, fill my soul with holy joy, courage and strength to serve you. Enkindle your love in my heart and walk with me along the next stretch of road before me. I do not see very far ahead, but when I have arrived where the horizon now closes down, a new prospect will open before me, and I shall meet it with peace.
Amen. (St Teresa Benedicta)

18. THE LAST WILL BE FIRST AND THE FIRST LAST

'Jesus said to his disciples: 'The kingdom of heaven is like a landowner going out at daybreak to hire workers for his vineyard. He made an agreement with the workers for one denarius a day, and sent them to his vineyard. Going out at about the third hour he saw others standing idle in the market place and said to them, 'You go to my vineyard too and I will give you a fair wage.' So they went. At about the sixth hour and again at about the ninth hour, he went out and did the same. Then at about the eleventh hour he went out and found more men standing round, and he said to them, 'Why have you been standing idle all day?' 'Because no one has hired us' they answered. He said to them, 'You go into my vineyard too.' In the evening, the owner of the vineyard said to his bailiff, 'Call the workers and pay them their wages, starting with the last and ending with the first.' So those who were hired at about the eleventh hour came forward and received one denarius each. When the first came, they expected to get more, but they too received one denarius each. They took it, but grumbled at the landowner. 'The men who came last' they said 'have done only one hour, but you have treated them the same as us, though we have done a heavy day's work in all the heat.' He answered one of them and said, 'My friend, I am not being unjust to you; did we not agree on one denarius? Take your earnings and go. I choose to pay the last-comer as much as I pay you. Have I no right to do what I like with my own? Why be envious because I am generous?' Thus the last will be first, and the first, last.'
(Matthew 20: 1-16)

REFLECTION

As is the case in so many of the gospel stories, there is a sense of injustice in this parable – surely the men who had worked all day should have been given more than the others? But Jesus is, in my view, master of the topsy turvy and, as in so many of his illustrations, there are deeper levels of understanding that he wants us to have.

I could pick out themes from this story. I could talk about the labour market, about unemployment, delegation, leadership, teamwork, fairness, equality, Dragon's Den or The Apprentice, wages and working conditions.

Or I could talk about God's grace, God's infinite, bewildering, visceral, sublime, eternal, outrageous, amazing grace.

Allow me to take this story literally to prove my point.

I don't know if you have ever been fortunate enough to work for a fantastic boss or if you've ever been taught by an inspirational teacher. If so, what were their qualities? Fairness, drive, ambition, tirelessness, being firm when firmness is needed, compassionate when compassion is needed. A good boss or a good teacher knows things about the workers or the pupils that they may not know about one another – or even about themselves. A good boss knows the capability and the potential of each of his/her team and the owner of the vineyard is one such boss.

This man is up early. He knows there is work to be done and he wants the best people for the job. I think he must have seen in those early birds a sign that these men had stamina. He knew that they would be able to manage a full day's work in the heat. Maybe he saw in them some leadership qualities that would be needed for later on in the day when the newcomers were brought in. Maybe you are that type of person. The fact that he leaves them while he goes back to the market place shows that they are independent. He can trust them to get on with the job while he's off site. Has there ever been a time in your life as a Christian where God has been off site? But you still carry on anyway – living out the life that God wants you to live. Some of the saints experienced years of not feeling the presence of God in their lives but continued to build his Kingdom. This is what it means to be a disciple, to trust that there is always a bigger picture, whether we are aware of it or not.

As the day goes on, the master goes back time and again to hire more workers – God goes into the places we don't want to go and brings in those whose credentials we might question. The Holy Spirit amongst us never tires of calling new people into a relationship with God – we see this in our own churches and in organisations such as Alcoholics Anonymous.

Not only is the owner ambitious for his vineyard but maybe he senses that some of the men who have been there for a while need extra support. How often do we feel the need to strengthen our faith through one another? God does not want us to stand still. Faith has to be dynamic. Fresh blood, new ideas, and an evolving church are always needed.

And what about the workers themselves? I'm curious about why those people have been standing around all day. Why weren't they up early? My first reaction is to think that they were lazy – you're probably more gracious than I am! It could be the case: if it is, that may represent a lack of willingness to work for God. The number of times I've missed opportunities to witness to my faith are legion.

But who knows? It could be that in this story the men weren't there in the morning because they had further to travel from home. Maybe they'd had a row with their wives or started the day shouting at the kids. Perhaps they had to look after a sick relative before they left the house or perhaps they'd been promised some other work which had fallen through. It could be that they were there early but the vineyard bosses didn't like the look of them; maybe they had a disfigurement or a disability which meant that they wouldn't be the obvious first choice. These scenarios are not restricted to this story alone. It goes on now, every day, on every street, in every neighbourhood, the world over. There is a horrible stigma around unemployment and I can only imagine the growing despair that these men must have felt, thinking 'here's another day when I will go home to my family and tell them that there will be no dinner tonight and that they will go to bed hungry.'

God sees that rejection. God sees that humiliation. God sees that despair and sense of hopelessness – and he sees it with love. That's why he brings them to his vineyard.

In any vineyard there is a variety of tasks to complete. The workers never stop! Some may do the picking, some the fetching and carrying, some the measuring; some may sort out the different types of grapes and what is needed for the final product.

It's hard graft with teamwork involved. There's delegation. Everyone has to do their bit. Each worker needs support and encouragement. The work is not the same for everybody and our work for God is like that. The author Helen Keller once said, 'Alone we can do so little, together we can do so much.' God knows that. I don't think that we always truly appreciate the creativity of God. There is a role for each of us and he assigns tasks to suit the strengths and skills of everyone. He constantly provides opportunities for us to grow and improve. Do we know this?

At the end of the story we see the owner of the vineyard paying the men for their day's work. Why does he start with the late-comers? This is why I think Jesus is master of the topsy turvy. He's not being mean. If the landowner had differentiated between the early birds and the latecomers, then he would simply be doing what we so often do. He would have widened that divide between the haves and the have-nots. It's not the way of Christ.

By starting with the latecomers this landowner is restoring their lost dignity. These men have had a bellyful of rejection; all day (and probably long before that) they've been overlooked, dismissed, cast aside. By putting them first in the queue, the owner (God) is showing them their value as human beings, restoring their self respect and letting them see that they are his beloved. Time and again in the gospels we see Jesus reaching out to those on the margins of society and these men are no different.

And in fact, for me, it's the 11th hour men, the people who come late to faith who have my sympathy – not those of us who have known God all our lives and have toiled in the heat. Why? Because these people don't know the freedom that God's love carries. They struggle on without the knowledge that this compassionate Creator of ours is holding their lives in the palm of his hand. They do not know the peace and security that such knowledge brings. We're the blessed ones because he's kept us close to him.

At the heart of this story is the unmistakable fact that God has no favourites. He is fair and just towards all his children. He loves us equally, no matter what. Our reward is eternal life – how can you improve on perfection?

FOR REFLECTION
- Where do you see yourself in this story? What is that telling you about yourself and about God?
- Are you unemployed or do you know somebody who is? Can you bring that situation before our loving Lord?
- Is there something of which you are envious? Can you ask Christ to touch and heal this?

- Is there someone you know who has lost dignity? How can you help to restore it?

WE PRAY
- for land owners and employers – especially those in poorer parts of our world, that they will be fair and just towards their employees
- for all those in difficult jobs – may they be supported by a good boss and compassionate colleagues
- for the unemployed
- for those workers in Christ who are seeking to build his Kingdom, especially those who feel that God is absent.

Jesus,
You turn our world upside down with your incredible love for every-
one. Help us to understand and emulate your generosity and to work
towards a fairer system of employment where the needs of all are met.
Amen.

PART FIVE

MOVING ON

19. *DO NOT CLING TO ME*

Now Mary stood outside the tomb weeping. Then, still weeping, she stooped to look inside and saw two angels in white, sitting where the body of Jesus had been, one at the head and the other at the feet. They said, 'Woman, why are you weeping?'

'They have taken my Lord away,' she replied, 'and I don't know where they have put him.' As she said this, she turned around and saw Jesus standing there, although she did not recognise him.

Jesus said, 'Woman, why are you weeping? Who are you are looking for?'

Supposing him to be the gardener, she said, 'Sir, if you have taken him away, tell me where you have put him, and I will go and remove him.'

Jesus said, 'Mary.'

She knew him and said to him in Hebrew, 'Rabbuni!' which means Master.

Jesus said, 'Do not cling to me, because I have not yet ascended to the Father. But go and find the brothers and tell them, 'I am ascending to my Father and your Father, to my God and your God.'

So Mary of Magdala went and told the disciples that she had seen the Lord and that he had said these things to her.

(John 20:11-18)

REFLECTION
In John's gospel, Mary of Magdala was the first to see Jesus after his resurrection. Why her, I wonder?

The town of Magdala was known as a place famous for its purple dye trade. For Mary to have had the name of the town put with her own name may suggest that she was a woman of wealth and could well have supported Jesus financially throughout his ministry. Regardless of her wealth, Mary was still a woman, deemed less important in the eyes of society. But not so for Jesus; his love was all inclusive and I like to think that this was his way of acknowledging her place and giving her dignity as a child of God.

Mary had been a faithful disciple of Jesus and had followed her master to Golgotha, the Place of the Skull. Mary would undoubtedly have heard of his arrest and I'm certain that this news would have frightened and upset her. After all, she would have known what happens to those outside the law and what the consequences would be. Mary would have seen Jesus brought before the crowd, bound, shackled and wearing the crown of thorns. She would have known of or have witnessed his scourging, listened to the crowd baying for his blood, seen him stagger and fall under the weight of the cross and stood by helplessly as he breathed his last.

Mary saw first-hand the ignominious death of her Lord, brutal and wicked. She saw him endure the cruelty in silence, punctuated only by words of love, mercy, healing and forgiveness.

How must Mary have felt? Powerless, afraid, heartbroken? And yet how much courage did it take for this woman to walk with Christ to his death? And now that she can show her love for the final time, that opportunity is denied her. There is no body to anoint for burial, no chance to perform this one last service for the master who has accepted and loved her totally and implicitly.

No wonder Mary is weeping.

We read that Mary stayed outside the tomb. Why did she stay? Peter and John had arrived, seen, believed and gone home. But some unseen force was compelling Mary to remain there. In the first sentence of this passage, John puts Mary outside the tomb; however, she then bends over to look inside. I believe that this is deeply symbolic, because any relationship with the Risen Jesus always takes us within ourselves. Jesus' call is an invitation to go deeper, not to keep everything on an external level, but to see the God who dwells in the heart and soul of every human. Jesus beckons all of us to look at the emptiness within ourselves and to see that his abiding and transforming love can bring joy, optimism, hope and resurrection. Maybe this is what the angels represent, that death will never have the final say; that belongs to God.

I also believe that in all the time Mary had spent with Jesus, she had learnt to listen to the still, small voice of God, inviting her to believe the impossible. Perhaps she had also learned to wait. Just because God doesn't appear to respond instantly to our prayers and answer them in the way we ask or want him to, does not mean they go unheard.

The angels ask her why she is weeping. I love this part. John's gospel is written with infinitesimal tenderness. The simple act of asking 'why?' gives Mary permission to pour out her sadness and despair. In my counselling work, I have often found the question 'why are you weeping?' to be incredibly powerful. It can touch deep psychological wounds; it can give people the opportunity to hear themselves say out loud all that they have buried within, often for years. This question provides the opportunity for clients to confront the dark side of themselves and to come out into the light of mercy and healing.

Mary's response to this question is a cry of anguish, expressing from deep within all her shattered dreams.

'They've taken my Lord away and I don't know where they have put him.'

Where do we put Jesus? Sometimes we take the Lord away and put him somewhere else. Fear, embarrassment, frustration, anger or self-will can cause us to hide Jesus away, to put him out of sight. I know that there have been many times in my life when I have denied the presence of Christ because the challenge to love as he loves has simply been too much.

But Jesus will always come and find us, just as he does here – not in a flash of blinding light or a blaze of glory, but gently, unobtrusively. Here he comes as a humble gardener. And once again Mary is asked, 'Woman, why are you weeping?' This is coupled with a second question, 'Who are you looking for?'

So many things can blind us to the presence of Jesus in our midst. Maybe we only see what we are looking for. Do we, for example, see the face of Christ in our brothers and sisters, in our colleagues or neighbours, in those we encounter on the bus, in the shops, on the streets? Do we see Jesus in the poor and the marginalised? Can we recognise Our Lord in the disabled, the sick and the dying, in the homeless or the prisoner? Do we even know that Christ is to be found not only in church but in the ordinary everyday business of our lives?

Who are you looking for?

At the beginning of John's gospel (John 1:38), Jesus asks 'What are you looking for?' Is it not the same thing? Is Jesus not the Alpha and the Omega, the beginning and the end, the answer to our heart's deepest desire? I think he is.

But the beautiful part of this story for me is that Mary recognised Jesus when she heard him call her name. 'Mary.' And her response, 'Rabbuni'. This simple two word exchange is so significant, so profound. Think about it. What else needs to be said but that? Jesus doesn't need any longwinded explanations of what we want, our shopping list of needs. Just an exchange of names is all it takes. We complicate it; he keeps it simple.

And again, look how Mary is drawn into this deeper personal relationship. She begins outside the tomb and then looks inside. At first Jesus calls her 'woman' and then he calls her name, 'Mary'. From the external to the internal; from the impersonal to the personal. Stunning!

I believe that there is a call here for all of us, to allow Jesus to call us by our name so that we can enter into a deeper fellowship with him, so that we can allow him to be our master, our teacher. Jesus then instructs her not to cling to him, not to hold on to what was, but to enter into a new relationship, a new life with this risen Lord. If we cling to someone or to something, we can never truly be free. If Mary is only looking for the dead body of a crucified Jesus, then she can never know the victory of the cross and grave; she can never enter into the life-giving power of his wondrous love.

'Go', Jesus tells her; 'go and tell the brothers that I am ascending to my Father and your Father, to my God and your God.'

So Mary of Magdala went and told the disciples that she had seen the Lord and that he had said these things to her.

Faith cannot stand still. John's resurrection story is not one of clinging to the old ways; it demands a fresh, dynamic response. The whole of this beautiful scene tells us that death is not the end, that Jesus will come out of the tomb to meet us just as we are, that when we open the eyes of our hearts and minds we will see and recognise him, that our loving Saviour calls each of us by name to an intimate and personal relationship with him, that in the tombs of our experiences, our disappointments and failures, Christ is there to offer a new and richer beginning and that once we have tasted the joy of the resurrection we are invited to share the good news with our brothers and sisters.

'Love so amazing, so divine demands my soul, my life, my all.' (Isaac Watts: When I survey the wondrous cross)

FOR PERSONAL REFLECTION
- What does Jesus' resurrection mean to you?
- Are you clinging to something or to someone? Do you need to ask for the grace to let go?
- Where do you look for Jesus? Can you see him in the faces of those around you?
- What makes you weep? Do you need to ask for God's healing?
- Jesus wants to call you by your name. Will you allow him to do this?

WE PRAY
- for all who mourn the loss of a loved one
- for the times when we hide Our Lord away and prevent others from knowing him. Help us to proclaim your Kingdom with courage
- for the willingness to spend time with the Lord, listening to him, talking to him and responding to his call to spread the Good News

- for all those who are afraid of what the future may hold. Lord, give us the grace to trust that you know what's best for each of us.

Lord,
Thank you that you chose Mary of Magdala to be among the first to witness your resurrection. Help us to see, even in our brokenness, our doubt, our sorrow and our despair, that you can use us to be ambassadors of the gospel and purveyors of your love and mercy.
Amen.

20. *I'M GOING FISHING!*

Afterwards Jesus appeared again to his disciples, by the Sea of Galilee. It happened this way: Simon Peter, Thomas, Nathanael from Cana in Galilee, the sons of Zebedee, and two other disciples were together. 'I'm going fishing,' Simon Peter told them, and they said, 'We'll go with you.' So they went out and got into the boat, but that night they caught nothing.

Early in the morning, Jesus stood on the shore, but the disciples did not realise that it was Jesus.

He called out to them, 'Friends, haven't you any fish?'

'No,' they answered.

He said, 'Throw your net on the right side of the boat and you will find some.' When they did, they were unable to haul the net in because of the large number of fish.

Then the disciple whom Jesus loved said to Peter, 'It is the Lord!' As soon as Simon Peter heard him say, 'It is the Lord,' he wrapped his outer garment around him (for he had taken it off) and jumped into the water. The other disciples followed in the boat, towing the net full of fish, for they were not far from shore, about a hundred yards. When they landed, they saw a fire of burning coals there with fish on it, and some bread.

Jesus said to them, 'Bring some of the fish you have just caught.' So Simon Peter climbed back into the boat and dragged the net ashore. It was full of large fish, 153, but even with so many the net was not torn. Jesus said to them, 'Come and have breakfast.' None of the disciples dared ask him, 'Who are you?' They knew it was the Lord. Jesus came, took the bread and gave it to them, and did the same with the fish. This was now the third time Jesus appeared to his disciples after he was raised from the dead.'

(John 21:1-14)

REFLECTION

I wonder if you have ever been on a fishing boat. I have twice, once as a teenager and once as an adult. Both occasions were off the coast of Ireland where the sea was rough and choppy and I was violently sick! I take my hat off to anyone who could do that for a living, especially if they go out and catch nothing. It's 'terra firma' all the way for me!

This last section of John's gospel is so beautiful in its simplicity. Prior to this we've had all the drama of Holy Week, the arrest of Jesus, his long walk to Calvary, the desertion of his disciples, the cruel brutality of his crucifixion, followed by his mysterious resurrection. Since that morning Jesus has appeared to Mary of Magdala, to some of the disciples on the road to Emmaus and to Thomas and the twelve.

I can only imagine the confusion and bewilderment of the disciples – so much to take in. First Jesus is dead and then he's alive. Then he appears to some but not to others. He seems to be coming and going, not fully present but not fully absent either. It's mystifying!

So what does Peter do? He announces he's going fishing. What do you do when you're stressed? How do you respond when faced with a conundrum that you just can't solve? A friend of mine makes jam. So often, in times of uncertainty and doubt we go back to what's familiar, to the recognisable aspects of our lives and that is exactly what Simon Peter does here. He goes back to what he knows, to where he feels comfortable and in control. Maybe these words have a deeper significance in that Peter was actually saying 'I'm reverting to my old life, the life I knew when things were more simple and straightforward.' Change can so often bring unrest.

And so these gospel characters are no different to us. When change happens and things go wrong, it's easy to be nostalgic about the old days, wishing things were the way they used to be when life seemed less complex. These stories continue to speak to us through time and space, offering us reassurance and solace. How comforting is it to know that whatever we are experiencing and feeling in our lives and our relationships, somebody has already been there? I find it immeasurably consoling.

Sadly, Peter's efforts do not have the desired effect. The initial haul brings nothing; not one single fish was caught in a lake teeming with life. It's only when Jesus tells them to swap the nets to the other side of the boat that their efforts bear fruit, or in this case fish! The story is so rich and beautiful in its symbolism. Because what it's saying to me is that so often we look in the wrong places for what we want or need. How many times do we seek consolation in work, food, alcohol, drugs, retail therapy, in meaningless activities or in unhealthy relationships? How often do we fail to see Jesus, standing by the lake of our lives, waiting to call out, longing for us to turn to him, to trust that all will be well? Maybe for Peter, his failure to catch anything, coupled with the reappearance of Jesus, was exactly what he needed, the nudge – the reminder that with God all things are possible. When all seems lost, God can and does intervene in a very powerful way.

We read that the net then became so full that the disciples were unable to pull it back in. Here we have a simple reminder of the generosity of Christ, like the wedding feast of Cana or the feeding of the 5,000. His bounteousness never ends, it even reaches beyond death.

What surprises me is that the disciples did not recognise Jesus straight away. How can you have spent three years in some-body's company and not realise who he was? Surely there weren't that many people on the beach? Surely the sun wasn't that bright? If they could hear him surely they could see him? It's perplexing.

I wonder if it's because they weren't looking for their master. They weren't open to the possibility that Jesus was there along-side them, their friend? They thought they were on their own now. Unlike little children who are endlessly hopeful and observant, the despondency and hopelessness of adulthood had set in. So often, we can see the crucifixion as the end. Are we Good Friday Christians or Easter Sunday Christians? It's a question worth considering.

I believe too that the Risen Christ is forever calling us to see him in a new way. Not only that, but maybe he's calling us to see ourselves in a new way. Death can often alter our identity; I'm no longer a daughter, a nephew, a spouse, a friend, a disciple.

But there is always new life beyond death and it is the new and risen Christ who greets us, welcomes us and holds us in our uncertainty and fear.

Sometimes it's so easy to lose sight of Jesus. It can be classic human behaviour – to forget all about God and to think we know it all, (the disciples were experienced fishermen, after all). What help and guidance did they need? The answer is that all our lives are enriched if we are open to Jesus at all times, when we feel scared and vulnerable as well as when we feel secure. We are never on our own. How reassuring is that? However challenging and disheartening the situation, Jesus is close to us.

I once heard Father Eamonn Mulcahy say that when Jesus died, every bit of him was taken up; only the grave clothes remained. And when he appeared to Mary of Magdala she didn't recognise him but thought he was the gardener. The disciples on the road to Emmaus didn't recognise him either. Jesus' appearance was utterly transformed in and by his resurrection. But the essence of him remained. What is that essence? I believe that John, the Beloved Disciple recognised the Lord by his ease, his care and concern for the wellbeing of his friends, his generosity, his clear direction, his simplicity and his love. Jesus comes to find each of them in their confusion and doubt; Jesus comes to find them in their grief and in their joy; Jesus comes to find them in the ordinary, everyday busyness of their lives.

Not only does Jesus come to find his beloved friends, he feeds them too. How considerate is Jesus to prepare a meal for these hungry, tired men? His thoughtfulness breaks my heart with its beauty. Could there be a more perfect Eucharistic breakfast than bread and fish on a beach, cooked by Jesus himself, a reminder of the feeding of the 5,000? He feeds them not just on the food he has brought, but invites them to bring their offerings along too. This is exactly what Jesus does in the mass, inviting us to share our lives with him.

Peter, ever the impetuous one, jumps from the boat whilst the others take a little longer to reach the Lord. Again, the symbolism blows me away. Because this ever-patient God of ours will always wait, no matter how long we need.

John tells us that 153 fish were caught. Did you know that in the four gospels, a grand total of 153 people were personally touched and healed by Christ?

And despite the number, the net did not tear. For me this symbolises the strength of Christ's ministry. Jesus will never let go of you or of me.

Do you believe that Jesus cares for you as much as he cared for his beloved disciples? You are as precious to him as each one of them was. Do you know that?

This story is so unassuming, so touching. It's yet another example of the presence of the risen Jesus, this Jesus who comes to us in the ordinary, everyday story of our lives. No matter who we are, where we are or what we have done, Jesus invites, welcomes, greets and shares his risen life with our commonplace lives. We don't have to do anything extraordinary for Jesus to meet us; we don't even have to look. An open heart is all he desires. Keep it simple!

FOR PERSONAL REFLECTION
- Where do you see or meet Jesus?
- How can you recognise the risen Lord in your life?

WE PRAY
- for all who are searching for meaning in their lives, that God will fill that void
- for all who don't know what to do after the death of a loved one, that God will show them the way
- for all who despair, that God will heal and transform by the power of his Son's resurrection.

Loving and creator God,
You take all things and make them new. Take my life and renew it in
the power of your great love.
Amen.

CONCLUSION

I N 1982 THE NOVELIST STEPHEN KING WROTE A NOVELLA entitled Rita Heyworth and Shawshank Redemption, which was later made into a film. It is a mesmerising tale of two inmates, both of whom are serving long sentences for murder, their unlikely friendship and ultimate redemption. Towards the end of the film Brooks, a fellow prisoner is released after 50 years inside. He goes to work packing bags in a food store where life becomes too overwhelming for him; in one scene he is heard to say 'the world went and got itself in a big damn hurry.'

I'm sure we can all identify with this sentiment.

Our world is constantly on the move. One only has to look around and see how quickly things change. I often hear people say that such and such would not have happened in their day and that they can't keep up with the pace of life. Fashions, eating habits, technological advances, attitudes, climate change, politics, social affairs, medical science all continue to evolve.

And yet we can be certain of one thing: God never changes. Unlike Brooks' world, God does not get himself into a big damn hurry! His love for us does not and will not change. It is unswerving, unfaltering, unshakable, solid and true. God is there in the good times and the hard times. He is there when we rejoice and he is there when we weep. In sickness and in health, in prosperity and in poverty, for better and for worse God is there, in all things and in all people, a beautiful, benign and loving presence.

I have said this before but I shall say it again. There is not one single thing that you or I could do to stop God from loving us. We cannot make God love us more and we cannot make him love us less.

Jesus came to show us the face of this God; he came that we might have life and have it to the full (John 10:10). By his death on the cross, Jesus went to the end of love to prove how precious we are to God. If you were the only person left on earth, I believe that Jesus would still have died for you. I pray that you will always know this in the depth of your soul.

St Francis of Assisi asked, 'Who am I, Lord, and who are you?' God is our loving Father, we are his beloved children and his favour rests on us.

Allow me to finish with this beautiful prayer of St Paul from his letter to the Ephesians (3:14-21).

This is what I pray, kneeling before the Father, from whom every family, whether spiritual or natural, takes its name:

> Out of his infinite glory, may he give you the power through his Spirit for your hidden self to grow strong, so that Christ may live in your hearts through faith, and then, planted in love and built on love, you will with all the saints have strength to grasp the breadth and the length, the height and the depth; until, knowing the love of Christ, which is beyond all knowledge, you are filled with the utter fullness of God.

ACKNOWLEDGEMENTS

I would like to thank the following people for their help in writing this book:

My husband Hughie Hardiman, my friend Ann-Marie Reid and my cousin Annabelle Elliott for reading, re-reading, tweaking, affirming, challenging, supporting and encouraging me at every turn.

My son Kieran Hardiman for your welcome interruptions when writing got tough.

Anne-Marie Bailey, my grammar expert and proof reader par excellence.

Terry Thiele for designing the cover.

My spiritual director and friend Father Chris Thomas for all your guidance and loving support.

The community of St Peter's, Hazel Grove for your unstinting loyalty and encouragement.

Last but by no means least, Anthony, Alistair, Laurence, Amanda and Joe and my parents Pauline and Hugh Mitchell for bringing me to mass, sending me to a Catholic school and for showing me what love looks like.

Thank you – two small words for a huge debt of gratitude.

Further copies of this book
are available from

Goodnews Books
Upper Level, St John's Church,
296 Sundon Park Road,
Luton, Beds LU3 3AL

www.goodnewsbooks.co.uk
orders@goodnewsbooks.co.uk
01582 571011